The Transition of Nations

A TIME

FOR UNIVERSAL CHANGE

Written by
Rasheed L. Muhammad & Abdul Wahid Muhammad
Copyright©2012RasheedLMuhammad/AbdulWahidMuhammad

All Rights Reserved
2013

Honorable Elijah Muhammad • Minister Farrakhan Muhammad • Master W. Fard Muhammad

Brief history of Nation of Islam of the West

The root meaning of the term Nation according to Webster's dictionary is \Na"tion\, n. [F. nation, L. natio nation, race, orig., a being born, fr. natus, p. p. of nasci, to be born, for gnatus, gnasci, from the same root as E. kin. [root] 44. See {Kin} kindred, and cf. {Cognate}, {Natal}, {Native}.] 1. (Ethnol) A part, or division, of the people of the earth, distinguished from the rest by common descent, language, or institutions; a race; a stock. 2. The body of inhabitants of a country, united under an independent government of their own. 3. Family; lineage. [Obs.] -- Chaucer.

In Arabic, Ummah may also mean nation. (See Map of Muslim Population Beyond U.S., page 6)

In Ernest Renan's essay "*What is a nation*" he espouses: "*people who show willingness to live together in the present in harmony are a nation*". He also states, "*To have common glories in the past and to have common will in the present; to have performed great deeds together, to wish to perform still more-these are the essential conditions for being a people*" He means if people are willing to consolidate their past and perpetuate their unity and be governed together by consent, then they are a nation.[1]

"On July the Fourth, the day of America's Independence celebration, He [Master W. Fard Muhammad] announced the beginning of His mission which was to restore and to resurrect His Lost and Found people, who were identified as the original members of the Tribe of Shabazz from the Lost Nation of Asia. The lost people of the original nation of African descent, were captured, exploited, and dehumanized to serve as servitude slaves of America for over three centuries. His mission was to teach the downtrodden and defenseless Black people a thorough Knowledge of God and of themselves, and to put them on the road to Self-Independence with a superior culture and higher civilization than they had previously experienced.

"He taught us the ways of love and peace, of truth and beauty. We are being led into the path of a new spiritual culture and civilization of complete harmony and peace, one of refinement in the pursuit of happiness and eternal joy in the Supreme Knowledge of God and the Science of everything in life.

"**IN 1931, THE MASTER WAS** preaching this Great Truth of salvation when He met a man named Elijah Poole [later renamed Elijah Muhammad] in Detroit, Michigan. He chose him to be His Divine Representative in continuing this most difficult task of bringing truth and light to His Lost and Found people. For 3 1/2 years He taught and trained the Honorable Elijah Muhammad night and day into the profound Secret Wisdom of the Reality of God, which included the hidden knowledge of the original people who were the first founders of civilization of our Planet and who had a full knowledge of the Universal Order of Things from the beginning of the Divine Creation.

---

[1] http://ebeysoman.hubpages.com/hub/Analysis-of-Ernest-Renans-What-is-a-nation

"Upon the Master's [Wallace Fard Muhammad] departure in 1934, the Honorable Elijah Muhammad labored tirelessly to bring life to his mentally and spiritually dead people until his return to the Master in 1975. The Honorable Elijah Muhammad identified the Master as being the answer to the one that the world had been expecting for the past 2,000 years under the names Messiah, the second coming of Jesus, the Christ, Jehovah, God, and the Son of Man. When the Honorable Elijah Muhammad asked Him to identify Himself He replied that He was the Mahdi. He signed His name in 1933 as Master Wallace Fard Muhammad to express the meaning of One Who had come in the Early Morning Dawn of the New Millennium to lay the base for a New World Order of Peace and Righteousness on the foundation of Truth and Justice; to put down tyrants and to change the world into a Heaven on Earth..."[2]

In 1972 the Honorable Elijah Muhammad publically selected Louis Farrakhan Muhammad (born Louis Eugene Wolcott; May 11, 1933, and formerly known as Louis X) to take his place as leader of the Nation of Islam (NOI). His first ministry post was held in Boston, Massachusetts, Muhammad Mosque #11. By year 1977 the Minister was prepared and readied to lead the NOI. The apex of his leadership was seen in 1995 when nearly 2 million black men attended "**The Million Man March**" at his call.

The question is: Will Allah brings about a new apex? One wherein Black people—America's former slave descendants will have a state or territory of their own? If so, how many of us are planning for year 2017 or 2057 for that matter? If this idea is not in our plans, know that a Mighty God is the best of planners. Know that a new nation shall come to birth for the betterment of all people and then increase into a universal government of peace, which must also include Muslims.

---

[2] http://www.noi.org/about.shtml

Muslim Population Beyond U.S.

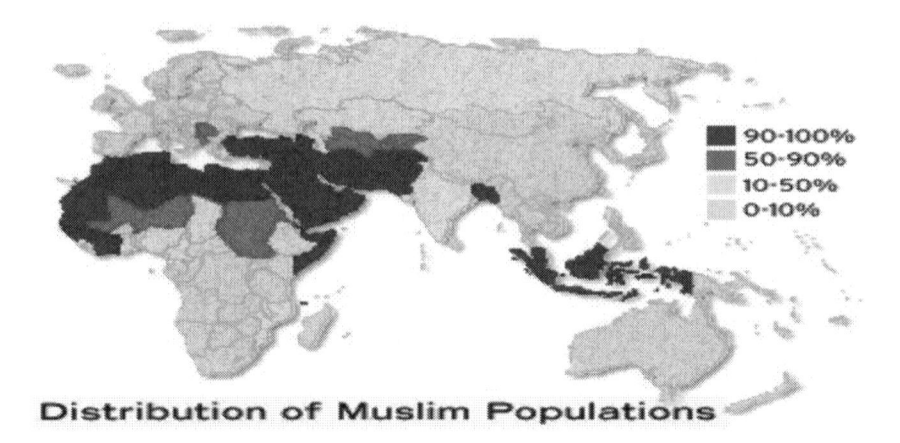

Distribution of Muslim Populations

The above map shows authentic information with reference to Muslim population in 2011 is 2.1 billion, which is greater than currently estimated 1.7 billion.[3]

In 1939, on May 26, the Honorable Elijah Muhammad informed his Ministers of Islam about a *Quranic* prophecy that will unite the Muslims again after their falling away from the truth.[4] The prophecy, he wrote, is contained in the following verse whose time is now:

> "And hold firmly to the rope of Allah all together and do not become divided. And remember the favor of Allah upon you - when you were enemies and He brought your hearts together and you became, by His favor, brothers. And you were on the edge of a pit of the Fire, and He saved you from it. Thus does Allah make clear to you His verses that you may be guided." (Holy Quran 3:102)

---

[3] http://www.muslimpopulation.com/index.html
[4] Ministry Class Taught By The Most Hon. Elijah Muhammad Vol. 2

Table of Content

OPENING STATEMENT 10

FORWARD 13

ONE 17

CIVIL RIGHTS OR NATIONHOOD 17

TWO 31
NEW UNIVERSAL GOVERNMENT 31
BRIEF HISTORY OF ELIJAH POOLE AND THE LABORERS OF ISLAM 31
U.S. FOUNDING FATHERS KEPT ISLAM A SECRET 42

THREE 45
NEW UNIVERSAL GOVERNMENT PART II 45
NATIONAL STANDARDS FOR CIVICS AND GOVERNMENT QUESTIONNAIRE ... 53
FARRAKHAN AND THE NEW BOOK 56

FOUR 59
NOI ECONOMIC BLUEPRINT EXAMPLE FOR BLACK AMERICA 59
NATION OF ISLAM BUSINESS REPORT 1974 61
WHY ONE BLACK AND RED NATION 65

FIVE 69
WOMEN AND THE HEREAFTER 69
SODOM AND GOMORRAH 76

SIX 79
THE CONSTITUTION 79
9 MINISTRIES 82
UNIVERSAL WAR BEFORE UNIVERSAL GOVERNMENT OF PEACE 89

SEVEN 93

BASIC GOVERNMENT STRUCTURE 93

EIGHT 100

MINISTRY OF FINANCE 100
POLITICAL SYSTEM OF OLD WORLD ISLAM 104

NINE 108

MINISTRY OF INFORMATION 108
MINISTRY OF ART & CULTURE 112
THE MINISTRY OF SCIENCE & TECHNOLOGY 113
DIFFERENCE BETWEEN STATES, NATIONS AND NATION-STATES 114

TEN 117

QUALIFY FOR POSITIONS AWAITING YOU 117

ELEVEN 131

FARRAKHAN MORE THAN A STATESMEN 131
RETURN OF FARRAKHAN 136
WHITE PEOPLE IN THE NEW WORLD OF THE RIGHTEOUS 149
LATINO'S IN THE NATION OF ISLAM 151

APPENDIX 1 157

MINISTER BEY MUHAMMAD 157

APPENDIX 2 159

BY ELEMENTS OF WHERE POWER IS HELD 159

APPENDIX 3 .... **169**

SIX THOUSAND YEAR TRANSITION OF NATIONS 169

APPENDIX 4 .... **174**

U.S. DEBT CLOCK August 14, 2021 12:07 PM … 174

END NOTES **175**

RECOMMENDED READING **176**

BRIEF BIOGRAPHY RASHEED L. MUHAMMAD................................... **177**

Opening Statement

I am so thankful to Allah for blessing me to be alive in the day of both the Honorable Elijah Muhammad and his servant the Honorable Minister Louis Farrakhan. I have served at practically every official position of the Nation of Islam since the 1960's.

My fondest memory of nearly 41 years in the Nation of Islam started in Los Angeles, California when [Min. Farrakhan] changed his focus from becoming an entertainer and actor, and getting back into the musical world and instead deciding that he would go back and do the work of the Hon. Elijah Muhammad. During that time, which took place in September 1977, I was with Minister Farrakhan in Los Angeles, along with Brother Jabril Muhammad.

In fact, after Minister Farrakhan took the seat of leadership over the Nation of Islam, I was the first to accept in the effort to rebuild the Nation of Islam. Thereafter, Min. Farrakhan gave me the name "Wahid", which means "first" or "one" in Arabic.[5]

The collaboration between Brother Rasheed L. Muhammad (whom I have known since 1985) and I to produce this book began on the Holy Day of Atonement held in Charlotte, North Carolina over a three day period. A part of what I shared with him was something Thomas Jefferson *self-styled* in 1820 based on his secret studies about the principles of Islam relating to civic duty and

---

[5] Final Call Newspaper articles Oct 16, 2009, MAR 9, 2010

government. [Holy Quran 4:148; 9:67; 9:71, 22:41, 3:104, 3:110, 2:256, 24:55, 42:38]

"I know of no safe depository of the ultimate powers of the society but the people themselves; and if we think them not enlightened enough to exercise their control with a wholesome discretion, the remedy is not to take it from them, but to inform their discretion."
--Thomas Jefferson (1820)--

The root meaning of discretion means "moral discernment and power to make distinctions."[6]

Other U.S. founding fathers also understood the importance of studying history, governments and an educated citizenry. Some said:

"..in 1787, someone asked Benjamin Franklin what kind of government had been devised for the United States. He replied, "A republic, sir, if you can keep it." John Dickinson, one of Delaware's delegates to the convention, agreed with Franklin completely. Earlier he had written: "Every government at some time or other falls into wrong measures.... It is the duty of the governed to endeavor to rectify the mistake." On December 7, 1787, Delaware became the first state to ratify the U.S. Constitution and accept its challenge to ordinary American citizens that they assume the responsibility for the security of personal liberties and the sound functioning of the government."[7]

I ask the question: Is there a transition of nations in effect and is a universal change underway?

In 1935, the Honorable Elijah Muhammad said to his ministers the following; regarding government and civics:

---

[6] http://www.etymonline.com/index.php?search=discretion
[7] http://www.udel.edu/dpi/ss/ssvii.html

Folly rather than History

DEPARTMENT OF SUPREME WISDOM

April 2, 1936

First: History is all our studies. The most attractive and best qualified to reward our research. As it develops the springs and motives of human action, and displays the consequence of circumstances which operates most powerfully on the destinies of human beings.

Second: It stands true that we the Lost Found NATION, of ISLAM, in the wilderness of North America have not applied ourselves to the study of History. But rather to FOLLY having a lots of the bread of, idleness and when an effort was made to the above affect of History study, it was to our detriment by not knowing what History that was more valuable, to aid us in the knowledge of our own Nation.

The WISE MAN, is the one who has made a careful study of the Past events of ANCIENT and MODERN HISTORY. The KNOWLEDGE of the FUTURE is JUDGED by the KNOWLEDGE of the PAST. There are MEN born with a gift of PROPHECY.

While some are trained into the KNOWLEDGE by intense studies of the PAST EVENTS OF HISTORY…

By Elijah Mohammad

Servant of Allah[8]

    This book merely represents a small treatment concerning why government is necessary as well as the transitions each must make according to the time and needs of their citizenry.

---

[8] http://muhammadspeaks.com/home/?page_id=743

Forward

In spite of many wanton criticisms about Reparations for Black America and the idea of our own system as others have established; namely, European Jews of 1948 in Palestine, and the Roman Papal of 1929 in Vatican City, this book is merely one paragraph of what is prophesied to come into fruition for the former slaves of North America. According to the word of God [Genesis 15:14], the original Scientists wrote: *"But I will punish the nation they serve as slaves, and afterward they will come out with great possessions."* Yes God has promised something great for the slaves/former slaves. Yes it has everything to do land and territory and no it want be pattern after what took place in 1948, 1929 or any other government known to this present world order of lies, deceit, corruption and murder.

Of course, the great prophecy will be only carried out by the Active Will of God Himself and His exalted Christ along with many wise and intelligent men and women of government, science, theology and otherwise who know the time and what must be done. The question is can America's descendants of former slaves' transition into a new nation of peace on some land and territory successfully.

The Honorable Elijah Muhammad stated:

"1. We want freedom. We want a full and complete freedom.

"2. We want justice. Equal justice under the law. We want justice applied equally to all, regardless of creed, class or color.

"3. We want equality of opportunity. We want equal membership in society with the best in civilized society.

"4. We want our people in America whose parents or grandparents are descendents from slaves to be allowed to establish a separate state or territory of their own, either on this continent or elsewhere. We believe that our former slave masters are obligated to provide such land and that the area must be fertile and minerally rich. We believe that our former slave masters are obligated to maintain and supply our needs in this separate territory for the next 20 or 25 years, until we are able to produce and supply our own needs.

"Since we cannot get along with them in peace and equality after giving them 400 years of our sweat and blood and receiving in return some of the worse treatment human beings have ever experienced, we believe our contributions to this land and the suffering forced upon us by white America justifies our demand for complete separation in a state or territory of our own."[9]

Can Black America truly represent new world of righteousness? And if so, will it be before or after the end of this old world? Do we really want to implement a goodly way of life wherein we all may enjoy luxury, money, good homes and friendships in all walks of life while we live?

In preparation for a new reality, all must at least study the example set by the Nation of Islam under the leadership of Minister Louis Farrakhan and Elijah Muhammad who actually demonstrated an example of

---
[9] http://www.seventhfam.com/temple/program/want.htm

nationhood inside North America for Black America and the entire world to see how to take *a poor nothing* and make something. A continuum and transition from Mosque orientated people, to community orientated people to Nation oriented people has been an expanding agenda since the founding of the Nation of Islam on July 4, 1930 up to this day. Another way to see transition in motion is like seeing a man go from Church member, to community organizer to President.

A transition is:

Noun
The process or a period of changing from one state or condition to another.

Verb
Undergo or cause to undergo a process or period of transition: "we had to transition to a new set of products".

Synonyms
passage - change - crossing - transit

Therefore, this book, "*The Transtion of Nations: A TIME FOR UNIVERSAL CHANGE*" shall feature some basic functions of Ministries in minute facets along with other governmental features, concepts, civic duties and a general question and answer segment. It will also provide common ideas about why a once lost people may transition into The Best Nation by God's Permission.

Rasheed L. Muhammad
February 10, 2013
15099

ONE

Civil Rights or Nationhood

No matter how and what America believes, the Atlantic slave trade fulfilled biblical prophecy.

According to the history of the Nation of Islam in the West, The Lost and Found members of the Nation of Islam in North America were discovered in 1930 by W. Fard Muhammad the Great Mahdi of the Muslims and Messiah of the Christians. His coming represented the expected appearance of God—The Supreme Being in flesh. We are not into a spook—immaterial what not. God appeared means: *"Come into sight; become visible or noticeable"* in fulfillment of biblical prophecy [Hebrews 10:5].[10]

"This man had to be prepared. He was not already made and formed. He had to be prepared a form to get among us. He could not come as He was, in the spiritual form of the Nation's mind.

"So His father had to prepare this man to come find us and then take us from our captors. We have to be taken. This is why that He, Himself, had to come. "Even I...", says the prophet, "..I will go after them. I will search the earth until I find them." A great lover with all power and with the eye to search the earth to locate that lost one.

"We are a very beloved people, for God, Himself, to come and search the Earth and the Nations to find we that was lost. We are greatly beloved for God, Himself, to search the Earth for us. That's a beloved people.

"He's so greatly in love His people that He threatened the whole population of the Earth to give them up. He said to me. He said that

---

[10] *That is why, when He comes into the world, He says, "Sacrifice and offering Thou has not desired, but a body Thou hast prepared for Me.*

if you had been here in the days of Muhammad (may the peace and blessings of Allah be upon him) he would have come and gotten you himself."

—Quote by Hon. Elijah Muhammad Saviors Day 1973--

The reality is Master W. Fard Muhammad's coming was first to Black America that represents the lost children of Israel or captives. What is a captive you may ask? Captive means:

1. One, such as a prisoner of war, who is forcibly confined, subjugated, or enslaved.
2. One held in the grip of a strong emotion or passion.
3. Taken and held prisoner, as in war.
4. Held in bondage; enslaved.
5. Kept under restraint or control; confined:
6. Restrained by circumstances that prevent free choice:

This is a perfect description of how Africans were brought to North America and what destroyed our people after serving 430 plus years living under white authority. Therefore, America—the U.S. Government has fulfilled and is fulfilling the final function of ancient Rome, ancient Egypt, ancient Sodom and Gomorrah and ancient Babylon all rolled into one.

These past histories and past powers were rehearsing a future prophecy that was and is being carried out and fulfilled by the *so-called American Negro (Black America), Nation of Islam and the U.S. Governmental powers and people behind its influence.*

1. What is the meaning of captive? How does it relate to Black America's 400 year sojourn in North America?

_____
_____
_____
_____
_____

You must ask yourself: Were Black people truly set free in 1865 and made citizens under constitutional amendments? Some say, emphatically no! However, the Civil Rights eventually gained in 1965 did enable *legal processes* to enable Black employment and certain other protections via *The U.S. Department of Justice.* For example:

Title VI, 42 U.S.C. § 2000d et seq., was enacted as part of the landmark Civil Rights Act of 1964. It prohibits discrimination on the basis of race, color, and national origin in programs and activities receiving federal financial assistance. As President John F. Kennedy said in 1963:

Simple justice requires that public funds, to which all taxpayers of all races [colors, and national origins] contribute, not be spent in any fashion which encourages, entrenches, subsidizes or results in racial [color or national origin] discrimination.

Between the 1865 Emancipation Proclamation *[free from control of another, but not politically]* and after the Civil Rights Act of 1964, Black America merely became a legal captive or lawful captive under the control and protection of the United States Federal Government. The question is: Did Abraham Lincoln free the black slaves?

"January 1, 1863

A Proclamation.

Whereas, on the twenty-second day of September, in the year of our Lord one thousand eight hundred and sixty-two, a proclamation was issued by the President of the United States, containing, among other things, the following, to wit:

"That on the first day of January, in the year of our Lord one thousand eight hundred and sixty-three, all persons held as slaves within any State or designated part of a State, the people whereof shall then be in rebellion against the United States, shall be then, thenceforward, and forever free;

*ONLY THE SLAVES OF "REBELLIOUS" STATES ARE ADDRESSED. AT THIS TIME IN HISTORY, LINCOLN ACTUALLY HAS NO AUTHORITY OVER THESE SLAVES OR THOSE STATES. THEY ARE NOW THE CONFEDERATE STATES OF AMERICA WITH AN ALTOGETHER DIFFERENT PRESIDENT.

and the Executive Government of the United States, including the military and naval authority thereof, will recognize and maintain the freedom of such persons, and will do no act or acts to repress such persons, or any of them, in any efforts they may make for their actual freedom.

*THE TERM "ACTUAL FREEDOM" IS SUSPECT, AND APPEARS TO MEAN THAT "EFFORTS" MUST BE MADE IN ADDITION TO THE PROCLAMATION.

"That the Executive will, on the first day of January aforesaid, by proclamation, designate the States and parts of States, if any, in which the people thereof, respectively, shall then be in rebellion against the United States; and the fact that any State, or the people thereof, shall on that day be, in good faith, represented in the Congress of the United States by members chosen thereto at elections wherein a majority of the qualified voters of such State shall have participated, shall, in the absence of strong countervailing

testimony, be deemed conclusive evidence that such State, and the people thereof, are not then in rebellion against the United States."
Now, therefore I, Abraham Lincoln, President of the United States, by virtue of the power in me vested as Commander-in-Chief, of the Army and Navy of the United States in time of actual armed rebellion against the authority and government of the United States, and as a fit and necessary war measure for suppressing said rebellion,

*NO MAGNANIMITY HERE. LINCOLN WANTS ALL TO KNOW THAT THERE IS NO LOVE FOR BLACKS AND THAT IT IS ENTIRELY A WAR MEASURE – NOT AN EQUALITY MEASURE.

do, on this first day of January, in the year of our Lord one thousand eight hundred and sixty-three, and in accordance with my purpose so to do publicly proclaimed for the full period of one hundred days, from the day first above mentioned, order and designate as the States and parts of States

*NOTICE THE TERM "PARTS OF STATES.

wherein the people thereof respectively, are this day in rebellion against the United States, the following, to wit: Arkansas, Texas, Louisiana, (except the Parishes of St. Bernard, Plaquemines, Jefferson, St. John, St. Charles, St. James Ascension, Assumption, Terrebonne, Lafourche, St. Mary, St. Martin, and Orleans, including the City of New Orleans) Mississippi, Alabama, Florida, Georgia, South Carolina, North Carolina, and Virginia, (except the forty-eight counties designated as West Virginia, and also the counties of Berkley, Accomac, Northampton, Elizabeth City, York, Princess Ann, and Norfolk, including the cities of Norfolk and Portsmouth[)],

*WHY THESE EXCEPTIONS? THEY ARE AREAS NOT REBELLING AND IN COMMAND BY UNION (LINCOLN'S) FORCES.

and which excepted parts, are for the present, left precisely as if this proclamation were not issued.

*IN OTHER WORDS, WITHOUT ANY AFFECT ON SLAVERY.

"And by virtue of the power, and for the purpose aforesaid, I do order and declare that all persons held as slaves within said designated States, and parts of States, are, and henceforward shall be free; and that the Executive government of the United States, including the military and naval authorities thereof, will recognize and maintain the freedom of said persons.

And I hereby enjoin upon the people so declared to be free to abstain from all violence,

*HERE, LINCOLN OBVIOUSLY FEARS RETRIBUTION.

unless in necessary self-defence; and I recommend to them that, in all cases when allowed, they labor faithfully for reasonable wages.

*"WHEN ALLOWED"? ARE THEY FREE ONLY TO LABOR FOR OTHERS?

"And I further declare and make known, that such persons of suitable condition, will be received into the armed service of the United States to garrison forts, positions, stations, and other places, and to man vessels of all sorts in said service.

*THEY ARE ORDERED TO GO IMMEDIATELY INTO THE ARMY. IN OTHER WORDS, FREED FROM THE SOUTH TO SLAVE FOR THE NORTH. A "FREE" PEOPLE ARE JUST THAT – FREE; FREE TO FARM, TO ESTABLISH HOMES, BUSINESSES, INSTITUTIONS AND COMMUNITIES OF THEIR OWN. THE E.P. CONDITIONS THE "FREEDOM" OF THE SLAVES TO A SINGLE ROLE OF MILITARY SERVICE.

"And upon this act, sincerely believed to be an act of justice, warranted by the Constitution, upon military necessity, I invoke the considerate judgment of mankind, and the gracious favor of Almighty God.

*GOD HAS NOTHING TO DO WITH THIS.

"In witness whereof, I have hereunto set my hand and caused the seal of the United States to be affixed.

Done at the City of Washington, this first day of January, in the year of our Lord one thousand eight hundred and sixty three, and of the Independence of the United States of America the eighty-seventh.

"By the President: ABRAHAM LINCOLN
WILLIAM H. SEWARD, Secretary of State."

BLACKS WERE NOT TECHNICALLY FREED UNTIL THE ENACTMENT OF THE 13TH AMMENDMENT, WHICH, BY ITS WORDING, ESTABLISHES ANOTHER FORM OF SLAVERY IN THE FORM OF INCARCERATION.[11]

1. How is the term "actual freedom" suspect in the above emancipation proclamation?

_____
_____
_____
_____
_____
_____

As it were, 100 plus years later, as a result of the Civil Rights Act, Federal income tax dollars were employed and are yet being dispersed to compel federally funded "job creators" to employ "so-called minorities" under a variety of legal compliance regulations in exchange for federal government tax incentives. By these means, the job creators may avoid being sued for discrimination and other civil rights violations.

In other words, Black people, under a *civil rights act* are contained by legal policy—not controlled by ourselves—but government figures based upon profits and losses and the avoidance of law suits. Essentially, we were made citizens under a legal procedure or compliance regulation via white authority allowing us to work and vote. Have you ever wondered why not the same for white

---
[11] http://noirg.org/lincolns-tricky-deal-the-emancipation-proclamation/
*NOI research group commentary

Americans? The bottom line is, you are either a citizen or not!

"A Citizenship denotes the link between a person and a state or an association of states..Possession of citizenship is normally associated with the right to work and live in a country and to participate in political life. A person who does not have citizenship in any state is said to be stateless." [1]

Therefore, to be completely free should Black America seek to lawfully transition self into a structure lead by themselves? And if so, should this system reflect what Master W. Fard Muhammad, referred to as a Universal Government? Do you think such a government will function in isolation and not interact with those whom have governments? Have not you witnessed the accomplishments of the Nation of Islam and how it has conducted business and nation operations since July 4, 1930? No one can stop Black progress except Black disunity and other elements of self-hatred.

2. What is the meaning of citizen and what is a civil right?

_____
_____
_____
_____
_____
_____
_____
_____
_____

Only a con or unlearned person refuses to acknowledge that Master W. Fard Muhammad, Teacher of Honorable Elijah Muhammad, indeed laid a base for new world of peace among Black America. He brought Islam to prepare them for self rule to operate in a state and territory of their own after 430 years of white America's form of government failed to deliver liberty and justice for all, etc., etc., etc.

Who realizes the time has arrived for nationhood under the principles of Islam, and not corporatocracy or disguised democracy? Has the time approached for Black America's own nation? And is it a crime to do so? Should not this nation be as such where there will be no civil rights act passed to legally enable anyone to work, live and participate in political and economical life?[2]

Most U.S. persons have not realized how and why the United States, as a constitutional republic, no longer exists. They do not know how America is an all-out corporatocracy ruled by corporate powers and special interest groups. In fact, the term "United States" legally means a Federal corporation under US CODE 28, 3002.

US CODE: Title 28, 3002. Definitions

"United States" means —
(A) a Federal corporation;
(B) an agency, department, commission, board, or other entity of the United States; or
(C) an instrumentality of the United States.

Clearly this means Black America under these terms is rendered powerless and symbolic without true government channels but limited corporate channels.

Hence, if a corporation becomes bankrupt, where do we go from here? Again, we ask, has the time arrived for Black America to self-govern under the principles of righteousness taken from the best of all scriptures, not corporatocracy or disguised democracy?

3. What is U.S. Code: Title 28, 3002

_____
_____
_____
_____
_____
_____

Economist Jeffrey Sachs described the US as a corporatocracy in his book *The Price of Civilization*. He suggested that it arose from four trends: 1) weak national parties and strong political representation of individual districts, 2) the large U.S. military establishment after World War II, 3) big corporate money financing election campaigns, and 4) globalization tilting the balance away from workers.[3]

In this corporatocracy there are no citizens, only legal fiction persons employed to work for very little pay. As far as those who are unaware living under this new world order—United States—a federal corporation, the U.S's financial collapse has occurred. Behind this corporatocracy is a small group of people called a plutocracy--rule or power of the wealthy! Under their satanic rule, billions of people work in what is called the "service economy" for very little pay.

Knowing this as a matter of record and fact, is a separate state or territory the best only solution for Black

America as God rendered as the solution to resolve the problems between the proverbial Pharaoh and the Children of Israel? Or shall we wait for a Balfour Declaration from the British secretary.[12] The point is: All past divine histories have demonstrated how and why any legal captive or former slave descendant must be completely freed indeed in quality and condition.

In recent times, European Jews were able to negotiate territory to build their own government base upon their interpretation of Biblical scriptures. This most famous event occurred in year 1948 when the state of Israel was formulated in the Levant (Palestine/Jerusalem), supported and financed by Europe's most wealthy Caucasian families ever to exist. Their premise was justified as to what they say happen to them in the way of suffering and persecution by gentile nations'.

What inhumane crimes have gentile nations' heaped upon Black America now going on 458 years. Do you think time has arrived for a new government structure; a structure governed and ruled by the Best and most qualified among our own people—the original people of the earth? Although Black America wants to play along with the political antics of white America, the Bible Isaiah correctly reported: *"**your agreement with hell shall not stand**"*. [Isaiah 28:14-19+ *" [14] Wherefore hear the word of the LORD, ye scornful men, that rule this people which is in Jerusalem. [15] Because ye have said, We have made a covenant with death, and with hell are we at agreement; when the overflowing scourge shall pass through, it shall not come unto us: for we have made lies our refuge, and*

---

[12] http://middleeast.about.com/od/israelandpalestine/f/me080508.htm

under falsehood have we hid ourselves: ¹⁶ **Therefore thus saith the Lord GOD, Behold, I lay in Zion for a foundation a stone, a tried stone, a precious corner stone, a sure foundation: he that believeth shall not make haste.** ¹⁷ Judgment also will I lay to the line, and righteousness to the plummet: and the hail shall sweep away the refuge of lies, and the waters shall overflow the hiding place. ¹⁸ And your covenant with death shall be disannulled, and your agreement with hell shall not stand; when the overflowing scourge shall pass through, then ye shall be trodden down by it. ¹⁹ From the time that it goeth forth it shall take you: for morning by morning shall it pass over, by day and by night: and it shall be a vexation only to understand the report.

Why is America so vexed against the ideas and teachings of the Nation of Islam revealed to them by Master Fard Muhammad through Elijah Muhammad and the Honorable Minister Farrakhan concerning a nation of our own?

In fact, did you know in 1933 Master W. D. Fard Muhammad was arrested for conversion"[13] Conversion means: 1. the act or process of converting; state of being converted. 2. change in character, form, or function. 3. spiritual change from sinfulness to righteousness. 4. change from one religion, political belief, viewpoint, etc., to another. 5. a change of attitude, emotion, or viewpoint from one of indifference, disbelief, or antagonism to one of acceptance, faith, or enthusiastic support, especially such a change in a person's religion.

---

[13] file:///C:/Users/Gateway/Desktop/Master%20W.%20Fard%20Muhammad%20and%20FBI%20COINTELPRO.htm

Conversion under U.S. Law also relates to common law tort i.e. "**A conversion is a voluntary act by one person inconsistent with the ownership rights of another. It is a tort of strict liability. Its criminal counterpart is theft.**" Here we should ask: By arresting Master W. Fard Muhammad, was the U.S. government admitting "they owned black people?" Did they see Elijah Muhammad's Teacher as some mythological ROBIN HOOD? And if so, then indeed He has fulfilled the scripture wherein it read, "*..for you know very well that the day of the Lord will come like a thief in the night.*" *(1 Thessalonians 5:2-4)*

Thirty years after the arrest of Master W. Fard Muhammad in 1933, the FBI on February 19, 1963 admittedly reported about **Allah**:

"In connection with efforts to disrupt and curb growth of the NOI, extensive research has been conducted into various files maintained by this office (Chicago). Among the files reviewed was that of Wallace Dodd Ford [Wallace Fard Muhammad]..It is felt that if the whereabouts of **Allah** could be inconclusively determined, the impact on Elijah Muhammad and his followers would be tremendous and could well serve to make Muhammad appear ridiculous (emphasis added – **WM**)."[14]

---

[14] file:///C:/Users/Gateway/Desktop/Master%20W.%20Fard%20Muhammad%20and%20FBI%20COINTELPRO.htm

The ridiculous has never been demonstrated like the FBI desired to prove against the Lost-Found Nation of Islam in the West!

I AM
Burnsteen Sharrieff Mohammed
Reformer and Secretary
To
Master W.D.F. Mohammed
...and these are some
of my experiences

[source: http://www.poolemohammedmichigan1.com/Items-for-sale.html]

TWO

New Universal Government

From 1930 to 1934, the early Lost and Found members of the Nation of Islam physically worked with Master W. Fard Muhammad (also known as the Great Mahdi of the Muslims and Messiah of the Christians). Sister Burnsteen Sharrieff Muhammad, became His secretary at age 16. (See photo on page 30)

The first group of Laborers (servants) of the Nation of Islam were positioned and commissioned to establish a nationhood structure by employing the instructions given to them by Master W. Fard Muhammad. He referred to them as Laborers of Islam. Each one was actually functioning as officials of a newly formed nation.

The basic ministry offices held during the early years were for ministers, captains, secretaries and the department of Education. Those first Laborers have been all but forgotten except one. That one is the Most Honorable Elijah Muhammad. He was best and neatest worker in solving the problems needed to uplift the lost Black nation soon after accepting Islam in 1931, just one year after Master W. Fard Muhammad founded the Nation of Islam, 1930.

Brief History of Elijah Poole and the Laborers of Islam

On October 7, 1897 Elijah Poole [Muhammad] was born to Marie and Willie Poole in Sandersville Georgia. He was the sixth child of 13 siblings. (See photo on pg. 32 of Marie *"Poole"+Muhammad)

Maria Muhammad
Mother of Honorable Elijah Muhammad

In 1973, Minster Louis Farrakhan was conversing with the Hon. Elijah Muhammad (HEM) along with a group of other Muslims all sitting at the dinner table of H.E.M. During that particular time, FARRAKHAN said, "Dear Apostle, one day..and I shall never forget this, mother Marie Muhammad, in this little room right here she said,

"'He *Elijah, her son+ is not the same man that I borned in this world.'" She said, "'Allah made him over with His own hands.'" And she was saying that you looked—in other words—that you were just not the same child that she gave birth to. That something had happened to you since Master Fard Muhammad had taught you. And to me it was just like He nursed you right up into Himself and made you to fall in love with Him so completely that you didn't want yourself—you wanted Him, and when you didn't want yourself---"

The H.E.M. replied, "..said that better than I could. That's right, Brother, He explained it right..And he's got it according to the Quran and the teachings of Allah and His Messenger...The Minister is a very wise minister."[15]

Minster Farrakhan finally concluded his comments by saying to H.E.M., "We love you, Dear Apostle; and I don't want myself—I surely want you!"

In terms of mother Maria Muhammad, her son met Master W. Fard Muhammad in Detroit, Michigan after migrating there from the south. He, Elijah, was the first disciple and first begotten of our spiritually dead people in North America to believe and act upon his belief. In brief, the true history of this event is as follows:

"On July 4, 1930, the long awaited "Saviour" of the Black man and woman, Master W. Fard Muhammad, appeared... He announced and preached that God is One, and it is now time for Blacks to return to the religion of their ancestors, Islam. News spread all over the city of Detroit of the preaching's of this great man from the East. Elijah Poole's wife first learned of the Temple of Islam and wanted to

---

[15] Table Talks of the Honorable Elijah Muhammad The Transcripts Vol. 1 pgs. 128-129

attend to see what the commotion was all about, but instead, her husband advised her that he would go and see for himself.

"Hence, in 1931, after hearing his first lecture at the Temple of Islam, Elijah Poole was overwhelmed by the message and immediately accepted it. Soon thereafter, Elijah Poole invited and convinced his entire family to accept the religion of Islam.

"The Founder of the Nation of Islam gave him the name 'Karriem' and made him a minister. Later he was promoted to the position of 'Supreme Minister' and his name was changed to Muhammad. 'The name 'Poole' was never my name,' he would later write, 'nor was it my father's name. It was the name the white slave-master of my grandfather after the so-called freedom of my fathers.

"Mr. Muhammad quickly became an integral part of the Temple of Islam. For the next three and one-half years, Mr. Muhammad was personally taught by his Teacher non-stop. The Muslim community, in addition to establishing religious centers of worship, began to start businesses under the aegis of economic development that focuses on buying and selling between and among Black companies. Mr. Muhammad establishes a newspaper, 'The Final Call to Islam,' in 1934. This would be the first of many publications he would produce.

"Meanwhile, Mr. Muhammad helped establish schools for the proper education of his children and the community. Indeed, the Muslim parents felt that the educational system of the State of Michigan was wholly inadequate for their children, and they established their own schools. By 1934, the Michigan State Board of Education disagreed with the Muslim's right to pursue their own educational agenda, and the Muslim Teachers and Temple Secretary were jailed on the false charge of contributing to the delinquency of minors. Mr. Muhammad said he committed himself to jail after learning what had happened. "Ultimately, the charges were later dropped, and the officials were freed and Mr. Muhammad received six months' probation to take the Muslim children out of the Islamic school and put them under white Christian teachers. 'This I did not do,' he said…

"His Teacher, Master W. Fard Muhammad, was also harassed by the police and was forced out of Detroit and moved to Chicago [1933] where he continued to face imprisonment and harassment by the police. In 1934 Master W. Fard Muhammad departed the scene and left the Honorable Elijah Muhammad with the mission of resurrecting the Black man and woman. [4]

   4. For what reason and year was Elijah Muhammad put on probation in 1934?

_____
_____
_____
_____
_____

Nearly 30 years later from unjust persecution and false imprisonment of the early NOI founders and pioneers, the U.S. government proved to not desire the public presence of Islam amongst Black America. *(See Appendix 1, Minister Abdul Bey Muhammad pg. 156)*

"Persecution of the Muslims continued. Members and mosques continued to be attacked by whites in Monroe, La., Los Angeles, Calif., and Flint, Mich., among others. Publicity in the white owned and operated media began to circulate anti-Nation of Islam propaganda on a large scale.

"Subsequently, television commentator Mike Wallace, in conjunction with Louis Lomax, a Black journalist, aired the documentary, "The Hate That Hate Produced," on a local New York City station. The documentary misrepresents the message of the Nation of Islam, calling it a hate teaching. James Baldwin, a famous Black author, released the book, "The Fire Next Time," based largely upon his interview with Mr. Muhammad. At the same time, white political leaders such as Senator Al Gore Sr., began to denounce the Nation of Islam and hold hearings on alleged "un-American" activities. Minister Louis Farrakhan and the ministers of Islam defended the Honorable

Elijah Muhammad and the Nation of Islam against these attacks in mass media in their public speeches, written editorials and other public relations thrusts.

"By 1964, Minister Malcolm X decided to separate from the Nation of Islam and formed his own religious and political organization. His very public defection from the Nation of Islam was based on his misinterpretation of the domestic life of the Hon. Elijah Muhammad Nevertheless, the atmosphere of rancor on both sides made ripe the environment for the secret police to meddle in the affairs of the Nation of Islam, according the late attorney, William Kuntsler. Mr. Kuntsler cited a declassified memo obtained through the Freedom of Information Act that revealed that the U.S. Government played a role in the 1965 assassination of Brother Malcolm X.

"After the assassination of Brother Malcolm X, the New York mosque was fire bombed and the Muslim community was reeling. Mr. Muhammad then dispatched Minister Louis Farrakhan to New York City to take over the mosque there and begin the rebuilding effort. In 1965, the Honorable Elijah Muhammad promoted Minister Louis Farrakhan to the post of National Representative.

"By the mid-sixties, Mr. Muhammad's ever-growing Islamic movement extended itself to more than 60 cities and settlements abroad in Ghana, Mexico, the Caribbean, and Central America among others places, according to the Muhammad Speaks newspaper, the religion's chief information apparatus.

"A host of Islamic and African governments received the Honorable Elijah Muhammad and donated generously to his mission. He visited the Holy City of Mecca where he performed "Umrah" (which is Pilgrimage to Mecca at a time other than the "Hajj season") during his trip to the Middle East in 1959 and advocated worldwide brotherhood and sisterhood.

"In 1972, the Honorable Elijah Muhammad opened a $2 million mosque and school in Chicago. During this important grand opening of Mosque No. 2, he praised and let it be known who his top helper was in his work.

"He asked Min. Farrakhan to come before the religious community and then the following announcement while digressing from his previously stated remarks: 'I want you to remember, today, I have one of my greatest preachers here-what are you hiding behind the sycamore tree for brother? (He chuckled)-c'mon around here where they can see you.' (A rousing round of applause ensued).

"We have with us today," the Messenger continued, 'our great national preacher. The preacher who don't mind going into Harlem, New York, one of the most worst towns in our nation or cities. It is our brother in Detroit and Chicago or New York. But, I want you to remember every week he's on the air helping me to reach those people that I can't get out of my house and go reach them like he.

'I want you to pay good attention to his preaching. His preaching is a bearing of witness to me and what God has given to me,' he declared. 'This is one of the strongest national preachers that I have in the bounds of North America. Everywhere you hear him, listen to him. Everywhere you see him, look at him. Everywhere he advises you to go, go. Everywhere he advises you to stay from, stay from. For we are thankful to Allah for this great helper of mine, Min. Farrakhan.' (Another rousing round of applause ensued). 'He's not a proud man," he said. 'He's a very humble man. If he can carry you across the lake without dropping you in; he don't say when you get on the other side, 'You see what I have done?' He tells you, 'You see what Allah has done.' He doesn't take it upon himself. He's a mighty fine preacher. We hear him every week, and I say continue to hear our Min. Farrakhan. I thank you."

5. What senator declared the Nation of Islam un-America and why?

_____
_____
_____
_____
_____
_____

Will the U.S. government encourage Black America to establish a structure and nation of our own? Can the once former slave descendants gain power to become a nation? *(See Appendix 2, Elements Where Power is Held, pg. 158)*

What is the meaning of structure?

1. Noun
The arrangement of and relations between the parts or elements of something complex.

2. Verb
Construct or arrange according to a plan; give a pattern or organization to.

3. Synonyms
noun. construction - building - fabric - frame - edifice
verb. construct - build - organize

While on this subject, what is the difference between a state and a nation? The concept of a "**nation**," refers to a large geographical area, and the people therein who **perceive themselves as having a common identity Government is broadly defined as the administrative group of people with authority to govern a political state.** A "**state**" is **an organized community living under a unified political system, the government**. When one considers Korea Town or China Town, you must consider how each is functioning like a nation with a nation i.e. within the USA. They know there common identity, they are organized with some form of administrative leadership and the system they employ keeps them unified. In summary, each is a reflection of its "own" government by definition of nation and state.

Every State consists of "**cities**". Every citizen should engage in **civic duties**. Some say the duties of good citizens are not easy to determine. So what duties are we talking about? Well every citizen of any good government is taught how to be organized and responsible in his/her conscience, taught the laws of his/her nation and trained to be family and community oriented. This is achieved by being informed how to contribute to your society.

Civic means, *"of, relating to, or belonging to a city, a citizen, or citizenship, municipal or civil society."*

In Islam, the indispensable civic duty of all Muslims is the doing good and preventing evil in self first. In principle, therefore, the paramount role of government is to create and maintain such conditions whereby its citizens and officials may know and exercise their rights to fully do good and be protected from evil in all social, political, commercial, media and financial forms.

Of course, silly thinkers say: "All Black people should think alike so they can live in their own nation; having a common identity, consisting of states and cities to live out responsible civic duties etc." But No! We are not all alike in thinking alike, however, we all need to respect structure and accept a common identity; and, that we were all created by the same Black ESSENCE of life! Then with the help God and the God-fearing, the principles of righteousness, not evil may be applied to nationhood objectives. Then perhaps it will be possible to transition into righteous government operations before we are forced to do so. One way or another, it must be done.

That's why; the Nation of Islam has been on a transitional course as an example in spite of naysayers, U.S. government agents and provocateur objections. Therefore, by the thousands, registered members of the NOI throughout North America are qualifying for positions awaiting them. By registered, we mean **registered** - listed or recorded officially and even those not yet registered are being qualified to bring about better world. [16]

So again, the question is: Is it a crime for Black America to petition to establish a government of our own.

6. What I.D. card do you carry to prove you are a registered U.S. citizen and why do you carry I.D.?

_____
_____
_____
_____
_____

7. Why is it important for government structures to request citizen registration?

_____
_____
_____
_____
_____

8. How do you define Government structure?

_____
_____
_____

---

[16] http://www.thefreedictionary.com/registered

Today it is evident that members of the Nation of Islam consist of people having a common identity i.e. NOI tenants and beliefs with an administrative group of people holding positions of authority and accountability. All registered Muslims are as good as citizens.

And what does citizenship denote?

"...Citizenship denotes the link between a person and a <u>state</u> or an association of states...Possession of citizenship is normally associated with the right to work and live in a country and to participate in political life."

Structure, accountability and membership within the Nation of Islam have been in place since the early 1930's. Detroit, Michigan is the first city where the Nation was founded. Chicago Illinois is the second city—it's National Headquarters and Muhammad University of Islam—Settlement No. 2.[17] So what is the definition of settlement in terms of nationhood negotiations and why was this word, <u>settlement</u>, placed in the NOI's Supreme Wisdom Book's Problem No. 10?

Think this over: As a noun, the word settlement means:

1. Act or state of settling or the state of being settled or
2. Act of making stable or putting on a permanent basis.

---

[17] Supreme Wisdom Book—Problem No. 10

In law, a **settlement** is also a resolution between disputing parties about a legal case, reached either before or after court action begins. The term "settlement" also has other meanings in the context of law. A settlement, as well as dealing with the dispute between the parties is a contract between those parties, and is one possible (and common) result when parties sue (or contemplate so doing) each other in civil proceedings. The plaintiff(s) and defendant(s) identified in the lawsuit can end the dispute between themselves without a trial.

U.S. Founding Fathers Kept Islam A Secret

> *"If a wife fears cruelty or desertion on her husband's part, there is no blame on them if they arrange an amicable settlement between themselves; and such settlement is best; even though men's souls are swayed by greed. But if ye do good and practice self-restraint, Allah is well-acquainted with all that ye do."* (Holy Quran 4:28)

The Founding fathers of America studied Islam in secret. For without it, America would be far behind.

"With more than 55 million items, the Manuscript Division of the US Library of Congress contains the papers of 23 presidents, from George Washington to Calvin Coolidge. In this article, originally published in *The Library of Congress, Information Bulletin, May 2002*, Manuscript Division Chief James Hutson draws upon the papers of Washington, Thomas Jefferson and other primary documents to discuss the relationship of Islam to the new nation.

"Readers may be surprised to learn that there may have been hundreds, perhaps thousands, of Muslims in the United States in 1776—imported as slaves from areas of Africa where Islam flourished. Although there is no evidence that the Founders were aware of the religious convictions of their bondsmen, it is clear that the Founding Fathers thought about the relationship of Islam to the new nation and were prepared to make a place for it in the republic."[18]

For this reason, the Nation of Islam was founded in North America in accordance with divine prophecy as you shall read throughout the pages of this book. The spoiled Western Hemisphere is nothing compared to what God or as some might say Jehovah Allah has prepared for the poor Black man and women of America and suffering humanity. The Holy Quran says, *"You are the best nation *as an example] for mankind. You enjoin what is right and forbid what is wrong and believe in Allah. If only the People of the Scripture had believed, it would have been better for them. Among them are believers, but most of them are defiantly disobedient."* (Holy Quran 3:110)

How many Muslims from Africa were imported to America during slavery? And since we who have awakened declare ourselves to be descendants of those slaves; only a lawful settlement will do justice for the inhumane act of slavery committed by the so-called new world settled in the Western Hemisphere. For that reason, must we reiterate the definition of settlement according to the law as intended by the founding fathers of America? *1*: the act or process of settling *2. a*: an act of bestowing or giving possession under legal sanction *b* : the sum, estate (land), or income (preparations) secured to one by such a settlement[19]

In summary, if there is to be a true new world, do Minister Louis Farrakhan and Black America have a position

---

[18] http://www.loc.gov/loc/lcib/0205/tolerance.html
[19] http://www.merriam-webster.com/dictionary/settlement

to fulfill in said true new world? Or is a feeble plan afloat to ruin what Allah has planned well in advance. [Holy Quran 8:30]

THREE

New Universal Government Part II

During the early 1930's, Elijah Muhammad was chosen by Master W. Fard Muhammad as the supreme minister over the Nation of Islam in the West. The instructions given to the early members and Laborers represented a transition out of an old world into a new world of Islam. The instructions read in part:

TO THE MUSLIMS OF NUMBER ONE MICHIGAN

"THE FOLLOWING is the Original Rules of Instruction to the Laborers of Islam and the TITLE OF MUSLIM Given by OUR SAVIOUR before HIS Departure, With a Footnote of a few words of Explanation to lay Pressure Upon their Minds of their many Errors in the Past and Present, that they may see the Light and Walk therein.

I thank you. Elijah Muhammad

INSTRUCTIONS GIVEN TO THE LABORERS

BY

OUR SAVIOUR, W.D. FARD MUHAMMAD

"The student must study his Assignment--Lesson #1. Each Student should copy the Answers of Lesson of Minister, Elijah Muhammad, and study until the Student is able to memorize, By Heart, all Answers to, of said, Lesson #1.

"NOTE: Here, Lesson #1 is said to be the Student's Assignment-"First."

"LESSON #1 lays the Base of our Work today; and gives the Student a Clear Knowledge of Himself and His Heavenly Home, the Best Part of the Earth; and who is the enemy to him and his Nation; and why the enemy and Righteous could not live together; and why was the "Righteous able to Cast Out his enemy. THIS Teaches the student what he must do with the enemy of the Righteous today.

"THE Righteous Nation is, now, Living in every part of the planet Earth. Therefore the enemy must, now, be removed in every part of the planet Earth.

"Why is Stress made to the Muslims to Copy, the Minister, Elijah Muhammad's Answers?

"The past History shows that the ALMIGHTY ALLAH sends Prophets and Apostles for the people's Guide and Example, and through them HIS Mystery was Revealed. And those who follow the Apostle's would see the Light."[5]

Can these fundamental principles of the NOI Instructions be used to teach the Original people of the earth a lesson, when we become awakened to the reality: We must have some land and territory of our own? In particularly, must Black America envision self as leading a nation having international relations with other civilized nations of the earth? [Isaiah 28:16] If so, what flag would we use to represent such a nation?

One example that answers the above question has already been demonstrated by the Nation of Islam of the West whose ensign (flag) was given to them by Master W. Fard Muhammad shown on the next page.

Nation of Islam Flag

This flag represents the universal creation i.e., the sun, moon and stars or freedom, justice and equality. Is this why Isaiah the prophet prophesied [Isaiah 11:12] *"And he shall set up an ensign (flag) for the nations, and shall assemble the outcasts of Israel, and gather together the dispersed of Judah from the four corners of the earth."*

Vexillology is the study of flags. Vexillology is taken from the Latin *vexillum* meaning flag or banner. One of the most popular uses of a flag is to symbolize a nation or country. Some national flags have been particularly inspirational to other nations and countries. Many national flags and other flags also include religious symbols such as a cross or crescent.

Vatican City Flag

Another example of vexillology is seen in the flag presented by Vatican City. This flag and city was established in 1929 to survive, at that time, the incoming new world order of Corporatocracy.

"Vatican City or Vatican City State is a landlocked sovereign city-state whose territory consists of a walled enclave within the city of Rome, Italy. It has an area of approximately 44 hectares (110 acres), and a population of just over 800. This makes Vatican City the smallest independent state in the world by both area and population.

Vatican City State was established in 1929 by the Lateran Treaty, signed by Cardinal Secretary of State Pietro Gasparri, on behalf of Pope Pius XI and by Prime Minister and Head of Government Benito Mussolini on behalf of King Victor Emmanuel III of Italy.

"The Lateran Treaty in 1929, which brought the city-state into existence, spoke of it as a new creation (Preamble and Article III)… Vatican City is an ecclesiastical or sacerdotal-monarchical state, ruled by the Bishop of Rome—the Pope. The highest state functionaries are all Catholic clergymen of various national origins. It is the sovereign territory of the Holy See (*Sancta Sedes*) and the location of the Pope's residence, referred to as the Apostolic Palace." [6]

9. Why was Vatican City established in 1929, and why did the Lateran Treaty see it as a new creation?

When we talk about government structure, there are many forms. Vatican City has been ruled by religious elite for over 1700 years. Their rule is defined as THEOCRACY.

Theocracy — **Rule by a religious elite; a system of governance composed of religious institutions in which the state and the church are traditionally the same thing. Citizens who are clergy have the right to govern.** [20]

So far we have exposed how and why both Jews and Catholic Christians, within the past 84 years, qualified self to negotiate for land and territory of their own to exercise self government over the international community.

On that note, I think it should be mentioned that an Islamic government in Senegal, Africa has also achieved similar aims. It is located in Touba and they maintain absolute control over their "capital" to the exclusion of usual state-run civil and administrative services. The founder of Touba is Aamadu Bàmba Mbàkke. He designed the cities intention after the original intention for the Holy City Mecca, Arabia.

"Touba is the holy city of Mouridism. Aamadu Bàmba Mbàkke, Senegal's most famous Sufi, was more than a spiritual master; he had a social mission as well, that of rescuing society from colonial alienation and returning it to the "Straight Path" of Islam. The city of

---

[20] By elements of where power is held

Touba played a major role in both these endeavors..Life in Touba is dominated by Muslim practice and Islamic scholarship...

"..For Mourides, Touba is a sacred place. Forbidden in the holy city are all illicit and frivolous pursuits, such as the consumption of alcohol and tobacco, the playing of games, music and dancing. The Mouride order maintains absolute control over its "capital" to the exclusion of usual state-run civil and administrative services. The city constitutes an administratively autonomous zone with special legal status within Senegal. Every aspect of its city's life and growth is managed by the order independently of the state, including education, health, supply of drinking water, public works, and administration of markets, land tenure, and real estate development."[21]

I reiterate, this is why for a very intelligent reason, the Nation of Islam clearly announced in Point 4 of *"What the Muslim believes"*—

"4. We want our people in America whose parents or grandparents were descendants from slaves, to be allowed to establish a separate state or territory of their own--either on this continent or elsewhere. We believe that our former slave masters are obligated to provide such land and that the area must be fertile and minerally rich. We believe that our former slave masters are obligated to maintain and supply our needs in this separate territory for the next 20 to 25 years--until we are able to produce and supply our own needs. [7]

Why not demand land and territory! European Jews and the leader of the Christendom (i.e. Pope) have

---
[21] http://en.wikipedia.org/wiki/Touba,_Senegal

received land, territory and nation-state status as demonstrated in recent history. Whereas they received their government status under white authority—*the* law of necessity—Black America must expect to receive land, territory, nation/statehood and government keys by the Active Will of All Mighty God, whose proper name is Allah. In this mind frame coupled with human interaction, our aims can be achieved. A transition into a universal government of peace fulfills all prophecies!

10. Name the 3 most recent peoples' to have established nationhood/statehood over the past 100 years?

_____
_____
_____
_____
_____
_____

According to what Master Fard Muhammad revealed to the Honorable Elijah Muhammad, Black people will rule self inside North America for 20 years. Is it possible for such an event to be fully established without loss of life and bloodshed? Well we are losing life and shedding our blood in every hood across America for no good reasons. Nevertheless, sadly, the answer may be no.

According to one of Elijah Muhammad's most trusted great captains and ministers, Abdul Rahman Muhammad, who wrote on page 47 of his book, "*I Walked With The Great Ones*":

"In those days, lectures were recorded using reel-to-reel tapes. We didn't use cassettes, and no one had even heard of a DVD or CD yet. So, one evening, all the Messenger's ministers had come to dinner and the Messenger said, ""I got something I want you brothers to listen to."" He played the hour-long, reel-to-reel of a brother who said he had a vision, and wanted to know whether he should come into the Nation of Islam or stay out in the world, where he should could better help the Messenger…After the recording was over the Messenger asked all ministers if they thought the brother really had a vision. Naturally, the ministers didn't know…They said,""If he had one, Dear Apostle, only you would know". Elijah Muhammad confirmed at that moment, that the brother actually really had a vision. The vision was about where he lived. The brother was talking about how the enemy would come against Islam and the how many they would kill. The Honorable Elijah Muhammad said at that time they would not kill over **300** of us because Allah would intervene and take all of them.."

What does this mean? What coast might this event occur, East or West?

Long time pioneer of the NOI, since 1957, *Emeritus* minister Abdul Wazir Muhammad experienced one such attack against the NOI in 1962, Los Angeles California. This occurred one year after he officially became a minister on the West coast in 1961.[22]

Many people have little to no understanding how and why the principle of what is called religion equals

---

[22] http://bhonline.org/blog/?tag=abdul-wazir-muhammad

righteousness first and foremost, not warfare, but strength to secure peace is one aim of "religion".

The Honorable Elijah Muhammad has taught only the principles of the present world of Islam will remain the same in the new world of Islam—a universal government of peace.

The 5 principles of Islam to remain are:

1. Shahabad (right way of life)Basic Morals
2. Daily prayers (salat) Cleanliness inward and outward
3. Almsgiving (zakāt)Charity
4. Fasting during Ramadan (sawm)Control what you eat
5. Pilgrimage to Mecca (hajj) Strive to give in to God while you live

But of course, you know what principle is and means:

Noun
A fundamental truth or proposition that serves as the foundation for a system of belief or behavior or for a chain of reasoning.
A rule or belief governing one's personal behavior.

Synonyms
tenet - rule - basis - law

National Standards for Civics and Government Questionnaire

By understanding civics, people can access power within the best governments toward upward mobility. Well to do this, civic duty is a must! So the Muslims, by the thousands, are qualifying for positions to conduct righteous government business for self and others? You should to the same!

Have you ever wondered where do people in government positions get the authority to make, apply, and enforce policy and law and manage disputes amongst citizens? Answer: by the **power**—*ability to direct or control something or someone* and **authority**—*power that people have the right to use because of custom, law, or the consent of the governed.* Without a structure, chaos prevails and the most vulnerable are abused. Therefore, civilized, mature and intelligent people dare not neglect understanding the following 5 question. If you will, answer these questions as best you know how.

1. **Why is government necessary?**
   _____
   _____
   _____

2. **What are some of the most important things governments do, what are the purposes of rules and laws?**
   _____
   _____
   _____

3. **How can you evaluate rules and laws?**
   _____
   _____
   _____

4. **What are the differences between limited and unlimited governments?**
   _____
   _____
   _____

5. Why is it important to limit the power of government according to the 5 principles of Islam?

_____
_____
_____

Yes, intelligent people have, will and are preparing to qualify self to conduct government rightly and function according to the laws of righteousness. [Holy Quran 2:177] Without a doubt, the Quran defined righteousness and if written in legislative policy and enforced, the entire world of mankind could be saved from self destruction, not to mention divine judgment. The question is: What is righteousness?

> *"It is not righteousness That you turn your faces Toward the East or West; But it is righteousness—To believe in God And the Last Day, And the Angels, And the Book, And the Messengers; To spend of your substance, Out of love for Him, For your kin, For Orphans, For the needy, For the wayfarer, For those who ask, And for the ransom of slaves; To be steadfast in prayer, And practice regular charity; To fulfill the contracts Which you have made; And to be firm and patient, In pain (or suffering) And adversity, And throughout All periods of panic. Such are the people Of truth, The God-fearing."*

Imagine if this one Quranic passage was ratified into law. How much better would all government services be? Why only an enemy of God (Allah) opposes such an idea to ratify or formally approve a better reality rooted in the principles of righteousness.

How many think a "new" universal government of peace must come into being and should we be the God-fearing at its head? After all, has not the Jews and Christians attributed this to themselves? Did they not once upon a time promote that it was they whom God chose to govern all the nations on earth?

11. What is the meaning of ratify?

_____
_____
_____
_____

Farrakhan and The New Book

According to the divine scripture and teachings of the Honorable Elijah Muhammad, Minister Farrakhan will depart to request his portion of a little book or new book (KEYS). This new book contains the guidance for the next civilization both bible and Quran refer to as hereafter.

The Biblical history of what is to unfurl concerning Minister Louis Farrakhan and the Honorable Elijah Muhammad is written in Revelations 10, "..**Go and take the little book** *which is open in the hand of the angel which standeth upon the sea and upon the earth. ⁹And I went unto the angel, and said unto him, Give me the little book...* "*And he said unto me, Thou must prophesy again before many peoples, and nations, and tongues, and kings.*" Christian scholars refer to that figure who **takes the little book** as an assistance figure to Christ also mentioned as a Lamb [Revelation 4-5]. So the Lamb or Christ takes the new book directly out of the hand of God Himself, first. Then the **assistant figure** mentioned in Rev. 10 gets a little portion of the new book to share that will establish a new universal government, world-wide.

Happy to say, FARRAKHAN'S next major assignment is spelled out in Revelations 10:8-11. When he returns, according to THEOLOGY, he will have the KEYS of a perfect government system, in his head, for all. He will have authority over the people. Unlike the early Catholic Church under its Popes, Bishops and Cardinals of old Europe, failure is not written for the Black man and women of America when the Rulership changes hands by Allah (Gods) Active Will.

<u>Big fields are awaiting for the wide Awake man to work out.</u>
<u>Arise the Dead by the thousands!</u>

<u>The dead Nation must arise - for the Time is at hand.</u>

<u>Look in your Poison Book.</u>

<u>Work cheerfully and fear not!</u>

<u>You are the Righteous, the Best and the Powerful.</u> [8]

The Muslim book of scripture, Holy Quran, says the community of Jesus will be made greater than all communities at the end of the world. It reads, *"When Allah said: O Jesus, I will cause thee to die (sleep) and exalt thee in My presence and clear thee of those who disbelieve and make those who follow thee above those who disbelieve to the day of Resurrection. Then to Me is your return, so I shall decide between you concerning that wherein you differ" (Quran 3:55)* The last Islamic prophet, *Prophet Mohammed ibn Abdullah of Arabia,* deep-rooted an interpretation about this prophetic verse centuries ago.

"How will you (Muslims) be when Jesus, the son of Mary descends amongst you and he will judge people by the Law of the Quran and not the Gospel..there will be no taxation taken from non-Muslims as to avoid embracing Islam..all people will embrace Islam..Money will be in abundance."[23]

Does the above mystic Quranic passage and saying (hadith) of Prophet Mohammed of Arabia represent Minister Louis Farrakhan's ultimate work upon his return? Is he the final factor of the "Jesus factor" in terms of his divine mission? Is he the final chain of evidence in the mysterious life of Jesus?

Be it Allah's Active Will, upon **FARRAKHAN'S** return from a death plot, a new righteous transformation will occur in North America, thus making clear the words of Prophet Mohammed Ibn Abdullah..*wealth will be shared in abundance.* However, a massive war shall erupt first, a final war to end all wars. [Revelations 16:16]

12. What is the meaning of transformation?

_____
_____
_____
_____
_____
_____

13. What is the meaning of Policy?

_____
_____
_____
_____

---

[23] Footnote: Holy Quran 3:55, pg. 76 of "Noble Quran" by Dr. Muhammad Taqi-ud Din Al Hilali and Dr. Muhammad Muhsin Khan. **Also see Yusef Ali Holy Quran pg. 137 Sura 3:55**

FOUR

NOI Economic Blueprint Example For Black America

Mr. Elijah Muhammad made plain an arcane and secretive technical vocabulary designed to awaken the soul of the Lost-Found original nation. His economic blueprint is a reflection of such science. The foundation of the NOI is built upon that science, which are five basic principles of Action and Deeds rooted in what some refer to as alchemy—the formulation of government and business operations.

An Economic Blueprint
By The Most Honorable Elijah Muhammad

"The Black man in America faces a serious economic problem today and the White race's Christianity cannot solve it. You, so-called America Negro, with the help of Allah can solve your own problem.

"The truth must be recognized by the Black man. He, himself, has assisted greatly in creating this serious problem of unemployment, insecurity and lack. Before the Black man can begin to gain economic security, he must be awakened from the dead and gain knowledge, understanding and wisdom which will enable him to follow my teachings. Islam and only Islam will point the way out of the entanglement of "want in the midst of plenty" for the followers of Islam, the true religion of the Black nation.

"Know thyself and be yourself. Islam makes a true brother to brother. If this be true, how can a believer (Muslim) be a true brother to another believer and boycott his brother and support the enemy? The believers in truth, Islam, must stop looking up to the White race for justice and take the following steps to correct this problem.

"Acknowledge and recognize that you are a member of the Creator's nation act accordingly. This action, in the name of Allah, requires you, as a Muslim, to set an example for the lost-found, your brothers in the wilderness in North America. This requires action and deeds, not words and lip service.

The following blueprint shows the way:

1. Recognize the necessity for unity and group operation (activities).
2. Pool your resources, physically as well as financially.
3. Stop wanton criticisms of everything that is Black-owned and Black-operated.
4. Keep in mind — jealousy destroys from within.
5. Observe the operations of the White man. He is successful. He makes no excuses for his failures. He works hard in a collective manner. You do the same.

"If there are six or eight Muslims with knowledge and experience of the grocery business — pool your knowledge, open a grocery store— and you work collectively and harmoniously, Allah will bless you with success.

"If there are those with knowledge of dressmaking, merchandising, trades, maintenance—pool such knowledge. Do not be ashamed to seek guidance and instructions from the brother or sister who has more experience, education and training than you have had. Accept his or her assistance.

"The White man spends his money with his own kind, which is natural. You, too, must do this. Help to make jobs for your own kind. Take a lesson from the Chinese and Japanese and go give employment and assistance to your own kind when they are in need. This is the first law of nature. Defend and support your own kind. True Muslims do this.

"Because the so-called American Negro has been deceived and misled, he has become a victim of deception. He is today in the worst economic condition of North America. Unemployment is mounting, and he feels it most. He assisted in reducing himself to his present insecure economic condition. You, the Black man, are the only members of the human race that deliberately walk past the place of business of one of your own kind—a Black man—and spend your dollars with your natural enemy. The so-called American Negro has never in the history of America been known to boycott or criticize the White man as he does his own kind. He thus shows love for his enemy and hatred for his own kind.

"A true Muslim would never boycott the place of business of his fellow Muslim or Black brother. A true Muslim is proud of the success of his Black sisters and brothers. He recognizes that their success is his success. He recognizes the law of Islam. If one brother has a bowl of soup you have half of that soup."[24]

Nation of Islam Business Report 1974

The Following are excerpts from the Economic Report given by a former National Secretary of the Nation of Islam on February 26, 1974 during Saviors Day. Even then, at the height of the success of the NOI, the United States—a federal corporation was feverishly working to reverse 44 years of what the NOI government and its citizens had achieved from 1930 to 1974.

As it were, in those days, NOI Secretary, Abass Rasoul reported, during Saviors Day 1974, the following words:

"A look at the accomplishments, established by the Hon. Elijah Muhammad proves that he is this man.

"As a foundation we have Muhammad's Temples in every city in America. We have Temples in Bermuda, Jamaica, Honduras, and

---

[24] Reprinted from "Message to the Blackman," 1961

even in (inaudible)... Educationally, we have Muhammad Universities of Islam in 46 cities. This man is truly building the foundation for a nation.

"In transportation, we have a fleet of cross country tractor trailers. The more modern ones.

"We have a fixed base operation air aviation department in Gary, Indiana. Now we know that America also has many aircraft, that are excellent in design and suitable for use, they are grounded. We are already in contact with America to purchase some of these.

"We are negotiating for the purchase of 2 or 3 cargo ships to carry across the ocean the various products purchased for our people in foreign countries. In fact, the first ship load of fish from the unpolluted waters around the South American country of Peru has already arrived in Mobile Ala. It carries with it some 1,000 metric tons of fish, or roughly 1, 200,000 pounds. The second ship is already on its way. This one will carry 1,200 metric tons. This will continue each month for the next year, at least. The only difference being that the poundage will increase.

"In order to be totally independent in this venture, the Hon. Elijah Muhammad has ordered the purchase of cold storage and warehouse facilities there in Mobile, Ala. negotiations are already underway, and we expect to spend at least $1,000,000 to prepare this facility for our influx.

"I personally can bear witness to the love, the honor and the respect the people of the world have for the Hon. Elijah Muhammad and the Nation of Islam. I have travelled completely around the world as the National Secretary of the Nation of Islam. And everywhere I have gone, the response to the messages that the Hon. Elijah Muhammad has sent me with were tremendous. In Japan, in Africa, in the Middle

East, in South America, they always respond positively to His program.

"The Hon. Elijah Muhammad is moving to establish trade routes across the narrow strip of ocean between South America and Africa. He is also moving toward China. In fact, I will be travelling to China very soon; the trip has already been set.

"The world of the Black man has extended their arms to Muhammad and we must be ready to grasp their hands."

"Note: The secretary went on about the deposit of $1,000,000 towards the purchase of the South Shore Country Club. 59.4 acres of land to be used for uplifting projects like universities and hospitals.

"By the summer we expect to have a fleet of pleasure boats on the lake, also a large yacht for movement along the Atlantic Coast.

"The Hon. Elijah Muhammad's plan is to build up the South Side of Chicago like the White man had done the North Side of Chicago.

"Had just completed the construction of an office building (the Information Center) at $1.5 million and the black contractor was told to break ground on the next. Business enterprises in the last year had moved toward $50 million in incomes."

During Saviors Day 1974, the National Secretary eventually summed up a list of Nation of Islam Owned Businesses:

"Salaam Restaurant, Muslim Import Stores, Muslim Fish House, Shabazz Grocery Store, Shabazz Bakery and Coffee Shop, Temple #2 Clothing Store and Office Building, The New Sales and Office Building, **Guarantee Bank and Trust Company**, Progressive Land Developers, Good Produce, Inc. , Chicago Lamb Packers, a National Trucking system, Aviation Department, Muhammad Speaks Newspaper plant which is a cold storage and warehouse, over 200 apartment units, also single family dwellings, farms in Michigan, Georgia and Alabama, over 150 Temples in North America, Bermuda, Jamaica and Honduras, over 46 Muhammad Universities of Islam, in the planning stage a 500 bed hospital, a new Islamic University, the Cottage Grove Redevelopment Plan that ran from 78 St. to 87th St., Renovation of Temple #2 and the University of Islam, the Phoenix, Arizona Development Project, Salaam Snack Shop, Your Super Market, Shabazz Bakery, Shabazz Barbershop, Shabazz Restaurant, Capital Cleaners, National Clothing Factory, National Furs Factory, Residential Homes. The 1 year circulation of Muhammad Speaks newspaper was 34 million copies."

The rise and fall of the Nation of Islam was written in the Supreme Wisdom Book, in problem 34. Allah (God) in the Personage of Master W. Fard Muhammad wrote about our fall and rise during the 1930's. He said:

According to the Holy Qur'an 59:7, the Muslims were very poor when they first started to Teach ISLAM and all contribution was given to ALLAH's Apostle for him and his Family's Support. And what the Apostle could spare, he gave to help take care of the Poor Muslims that were unable to help themselves and the other part was given to those who were confined to the Labor of ISLAM.

And soon, there arose an argument among the Hypocrites about the use of the money because they thought that they should share equally with the Apostle. Then ALLAH cast these Hypocrites out and punished them for the false accusation that they had spread against the Prophet, that he was seeking to enrich himself and acting unjustly to the poor and needy.

And, then ALLAH, told the other Laborers that HE would soon enrich all of them but, at present, every effort should be to maintain the Prophet and his household.

<u>The enemy, then, tried to stop every Muslim from helping the Apostle and said he should be killed. Then ALLAH Challenged the enemy to do so - to leave not a stone unturned in trying.</u>

<u>This is in the 34 Problems that you have, if you understand.</u> [9]

Many do not understand why the Nation of Islam fell to nothing (zero) after 1975 while others don't care. Nevertheless, within problem 34 is the time-factor Elijah Muhammad would escape a death plot in 1975; and, in problem 31 is the two years it would take Minister Farrakhan to receive key information he'd need before taking leadership over the Nation of Islam in 1977. So now millions thank Allah that FARRAKHAN was able to turn those keys in time enough to rebuild the NOI government structure for new generations to come forever!

Why One Black and Red Nation

Do we want to be seen as an individual or a legal person? Or are we or can we be a Universal Government (ONE NATION)—that is America's former Black slaves and Native Americans?

By this we mean, whereas Native Americans migrated to North America 16,000 years ago from ancient India and the black men and women were kidnapped from Africa and enslaved in North America 458 years from today, both remain politically feeble and conduct business in a tribal manner thereby remaining disunited under "*white authority.*"

For instance, in 1871 the Indian Appropriations Act was passed to prevent these tribes from becoming an independent nation.

"The Indian Appropriations Act of 1871 had two significant sections. First, the Act required the Federal Government no longer interact with the various tribes through treaties, but rather through statutes by stating, in part, "*n+o Indian nation or tribe within the territory of the United States shall be acknowledged or recognized as an independent nation."[25]

Thereafter, six years later in 1877 the U.S. Government *in the name of jim crow and black code laws* was instituted to prevent America's ex-slaves from constructing an independent nation after Abraham Lincoln's Emancipation Proclamation.

"In the different states Reconstruction began and ended at different times; federal Reconstruction finally ended with the Compromise of 1877. Reconstruction policies were debated in the North when the war began, and commenced in earnest after the Emancipation Proclamation, issued on January 1, 1863...

"This was followed by a period that white Southerners labeled Redemption, in which white-dominated state legislatures enacted Jim Crow laws and (after 1890) disenfranchised most blacks and many poor whites through a combination of constitutional amendments and electoral laws. The white Democrat Southerners' memory of Reconstruction played a major role in imposing the system of white supremacy and second-class citizenship for blacks, known as the age of Jim Crow."[26]

By jurisdiction of the western world, the Black and Red nation have been terrified by a hell-raising race whose control over land and sea has been hidden under legal

---

[25] 25 U.S.C. § 71. Indian Appropriation Act of March 3, 1871, 16 Stat. 544, 566
[26] http://en.wikipedia.org/wiki/Reconstruction_era_of_the_United_States

fiction via merchant law. [Matt. 23:15] "...*You travel over land and sea to make a single convert, and when this happens you make him twice as fit for hell as you are.*" This bible passage says much when one understands ancient history and our existing predicament since Christopher Columbus sailed the ocean blue, Sir John Hopkins promises that never came true, and *"white authorities"* enforcement of their <u>law of necessity</u>.

14. Why did the Honorable Elijah Muhammad say *"Stop wanton criticisms of everything that is Black-owned and Black-operated"* and *"Observe the operations of the White man. He is successful. He makes no excuses for his failures. He works hard in a collective manner. You do the same."*

_____
_____
_____
_____
_____
_____
_____
_____
_____
_____
_____
_____
_____
_____
_____
_____

The example set by the Nation of Islam is by voluntary gifts from its registered members and well wishers only proves her marvelous legitimacy and moral right to transition into an ever expanding nation with the best structure.

People power, decision makers and political action based on belief systems make transitions happen. Moreover, transitions of nations were all pre-written by the Lord of All Worlds to happen in accordance with time using people—men, women and children.

FIVE

Women And The Hereafter

Mother Tynetta Muhammad, Minister, Writer, Music Composer and wife of the Honorable Elijah Muhammad wrote in FCN, on November 14, 2012, the following:

"The Nation of Islam is a training ground in preparation for the Life of the Hereafter. The Most Honorable Elijah Muhammad shared with us that Master Fard Muhammad's Teachings to him covered three-fourths of the material pertaining to the Life of the Hereafter and three-fourths of his work directed to the woman…

"The study of history is our best guide for future evolution. The study of history rewards our research. In coming to this critical period of world history, I wish to expound a little further on the work of the angels under the command of Almighty God, Allah. As previously mentioned three-fourths of the Divine Teachings of the Most Honorable Elijah Muhammad from the Master was pertaining to the Life of the Hereafter, and three-fourths of his work was focused on the woman and her role in developing a new world civilization.

"Upon many occasions, the Honorable Elijah Muhammad spoke of the work of the angels in the Final Judgment of this world calling them the Executioners of God's Will. He stated that behind him would come the Executioners referring to these powerful beings and forces working under the Command of Almighty God, Allah." [27]

Regarding the final phase into the life of the Hereafter, while we live, was clarified by the Honorable Elijah

---

[27] http://www.finalcall.com/artman/publish/Columns_4/article_9360.shtml

Muhammad, on August 13, 1956. He wrote in the Pittsburg Carrier the following words:

"The HEREAFTER; there the righteous will make an unlimited progress, peace, joy and happiness will have no end. War will be forgotten, disagreement will have no place in the HEREAFTER. The present Brotherhood of Islam is typical of the life in the HEREAFTER, the difference is that the Brotherhood in the HEREAFTER will enjoy the spirit of gladness and happiness forever in the Presence of Allah.

"The earth, the general atmosphere will produce such a change that the people will think that it is a new earth. It will be the heaven of the righteous forever; no sickness, no hospitals, no insane asylums, no gambling, no cursing and swearing will be seen or heard in that life. Fear, grief and sorrow will stop on this side as a proof. Every one of us who accept the religion of Islam and follow what God has revealed to me, will begin enjoying the above life here."

15. Why are women important to bring about any transition from an old world order into a new one?

_____
_____
_____
_____
_____
_____
_____
_____

What the righteous shall be taught over a 20 year time span, by their own scientists, in the Far Pacific according what Elijah Muhammad revealed in his 1972 Theology of Time lecture series, will enable them to square the entire nations of the earth into a universal government. Once again, do you believe this form of government will do what the leaders of the white race, as a group, failed to do with all they have learned of God, his prophets and the ancients over the past 4,000 years; from Moses to Menes of ancient Egypt, to Hammurabi of ancient Babylon, from Solon to Draco, from Prophet Mohammed of Arabia to MUHAMMAD of today?

On October 20, 1956 Messenger Elijah Muhammad wrote in the Pittsburg Courier with regard to the future divine governmental work of the Black man and woman of America:

"144,000--THIS number is mentioned in the Bible (Rev. 14:1) as being the number of the first believers in Allah (God) and His messenger.

"The messenger is called a lamb due to certain characteristics of his (the messenger) being similar to that of a sheep, and the tender love of Allah for Him like that of a good shepherd towards his sheep.

"Though the love of Allah (God) for the so-called Negroes is not equaled by anyone. Describing us as sheep is about the best way of putting it, as sheep are dumb, ignorant and humble, not aggressive...

"THE NUMBER (144,000), in mathematics means a SQUARE which is a perfect answer for the spiritual work of Allah (God) with that number of people. They are the first (Negro) converts from among the wicked to Allah (God and His Messenger, referred to as the first ripe fruit (the first of the righteous) unto God and the Lamb, in verse 4 of the same chapter. They are righteous enough (ripe) to be picked out of the wicked race to be used for the purpose of squaring the nations of earth into righteousness."

"After the righteous black nation has labored under the wicked rule of the devils for 6,000 years, the return to a righteous ruler, under the God of Righteousness, the people must be reorganized to live under such government.

"The All Wise God Allah to Whom praise is due, Who came in the person of Master W.F. Muhammad, seeking us, the lost and last members of a chosen nation, is building a new world of Islam out of the old.

"Therefore, He lays the base of His Kingdom with a square number of MATHEMATICS TRUTH.

"His New World of Islam (Kingdom of Peace) can be proven mathematically step by step, which we all know that mathematics is truth...This number (144,000) will be made up of all the so-called American Negroes who have been the merchandise of the American whites for 400 years...

"The Revelator didn't see a single one of the Caucasian race in the number (144,000). "THE NUMBER 144, the root is "12" and there are 12 Tribes, the 12 Imams the real answer.

"Allah said we once had 13 Tribes, but one got lost. The number 144 will be the Stars of the Nation, and this number (144) multiplied by 12 equals a cube.

"This number (144,000) so-called Negroes, under the guidance of Allah (God) Who came in the Person of Master W.F. Muhammad, will cube the whole nation of black mankind, into a nation of righteousness."

Can the original Asiatic people and/or Black America truly be The Foundation Stone? Perhaps, after the final massive WWIII, the psyche of the minds of the people will be ready to transition into a Righteous GOVERNMENTAL Structure. If so, will the likes of Minister Farrakhan be present? Will he have The Keys of Government as it was pre-written in divine scripture?

On March 31, 1967 Elijah Muhammad wrote in the Muhammad Speaks Newspaper concerning a waging war and the Hereafter after such war:

"The people of Russia are referred to in the Bible and Holy Quran-an as the Gogs. Other infidel people, such as the European and American white race, are referred to by some of the scientists as being the Magogs. However, that great sign of God's work, in the Person of Master Fard Muhammad, is to teach us the knowledge of ourselves from the beginning of the creations of the heavens and the earth, declaring us to be the members of the Creator. We must be awakened to the knowledge of ourselves as being such members.

"This knowledge should force us to take our place in the sun and use the very nature and the law of that sun for our standard. We would have love for our government on earth as a freedom loving people and grant freedom to all life that is in the sun as our Father created the sun to give us light and heat freely. And in our dealings with man, we should give to him the freedom to exercise his well-being in the universe which is necessary for his well-being - freely, without hindrance.

"The white race has deprived the black people of this - and equal chance of freedom (although the sun and its planets by nature give light freely) and an equal chance to survive and share in the earth that our Father created for us all that come onto the earth-except enemies, as the white race. OUT OF the law of freedom, justice and equality, the white race was brought. The white race is an opposer of freedom, justice and equality. They were made, by nature, to oppose the freedom of the lives of other human beings, of beasts, fowls of the air, and fish of the sea.

"They have brought much trouble between men on the face of our earth, up to today. **Through the wakening of the people by the truth of Almighty God Allah, in the Person of Master Fard Muhammad. they have become so angry and dissatisfied with the white race as being an enemy to the well-being of other than white, that today a raging war now has begun**. It will have no end until the God of freedom, justice and equality has made all men to bow to the general law of nature. THEN, AND only then, will we enjoy our people on this earth in peace and love of the brotherhood.

"Our bodies have the fire of the sun in them.

"ALL OF this, which is essential for our existence, has not served as a knowledge to the enemy, devil, that he should have used the law of freedom in his rulership of the people of earth. Freedom is essential to life itself. What is life without freedom? Life ever cries and seeks the way to freedom. This is the nature of life. No one has been so evil to imprison life, but the enemy, devil of ours. HE HAS built strong prison houses everywhere under his rule to bind and cast into prison those who, by nature, are made free and should be free. **In the Hereafter there will be no jails - for there will be no prisoners to put in jail**".

It has been taught what the Muslims are to do before this war fully ignites that is a) store food, b) water and c) other survival supplies to last from six months to one year. When the worst chaos hits the streets, our homes may be a place of refuge. [Exodus 12:23] *"he will see the blood on the top and sides of the doorframe and will pass over that doorway, and he will not permit the destroyer to enter your houses and strike you down."* Last of all, according to the teachings of the Honorable Elijah Muhammad, when the war ends, an unhindered New Kingdom of Freedom, Justice, and Equality will flourish, which our Righteous Savior, the Mighty Allah is setting up.[28]

16. What is the meaning of Gog and Magog?

_____
_____
_____
_____

Will a universal government be rolled out or implemented around the entire globe? Are there really two phases of the Hereafter? Will one phase really begin in North America and the final phase transition beyond the boundaries of North America after her final Judgment? As for the none-understander[s], why does [Isaiah 13:14] read, *"Everyone in Babylon will run about like a hunted gazelle, like sheep without a shepherd. They will try to find their own people and flee to their own land."* Does this passage have anything to do with America's final Judgment? [Also read Holy Quran 56]

"Allah (God) will cut a shortage in gravity and a fire will start from 13-layers up and burn down, burning the atmosphere. When it gets to the earth, it will burn everything. It will burn for 310 years and take 690 years to cool off.

"The Book of Revelation says, And the Kings of the earth who have committed fornication with her, shall lament for her when they shall see the smoke of her burning. *[Rev. 18:18-19]* This fire is for us. It's

---

[28] Ministry Class Taught By The Most Honorable Elijah Muhammad Vol. 1.

prepared from men and stones. Stones represent the hard-hearted people of this wicked world and for men who refuse to change and come to God.

"You are in the valley of decision. What are you going to do? Are you going to clean up your lives? I'm not asking you if you want to join me. You can if you want to. But if you are in the church, you better make the church right because Judgment is going to begin at the so-called house of God. Wherever you are, you are going to have to clean it up. Whatever we are doing that we know is wrong, we must straighten it out. But if you don't it's on you." --**Minister Louis Farrakhan, June 9, 1996 at Mosque Maryam in Chicago—**

I reiterate, unlike the Caucasian race, which was also given keys of government in past times, but failed to rule properly; when Black America and members of Nation of Islam receive the keys, NEW KEYS, in science, government and in economy to bring about a Universal Government of Peace, her rule shall be everlasting! [Holy Quran 56] Not a one world order for globalization.

Sodom and Gomorrah

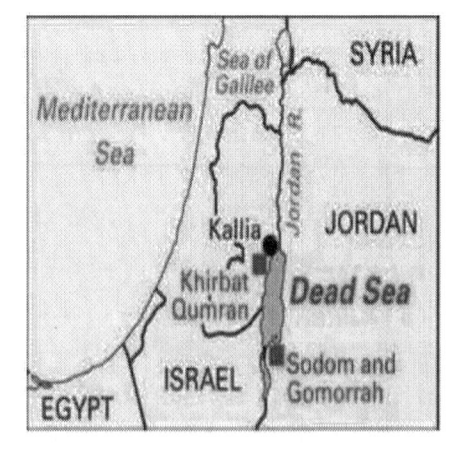

Bible Question: In what years were Sodom and Gomorrah destroyed? It was destroyed around 2067-2066 B.C. See Levant map below of region where the old wicked city once existed. [Gen 13:10] Most biblical archeologists believe the ancient ruins of these cities are buried beneath the water. And that it may have been the sulfur and chemical content within the water supply which made the people of Sodom and Gomorrah deviate from the norm over 4,000 years ago.

By and by God destroyed these two cities and their inhabitants because they were living what is now called an "alternate life style." The sin was homosexuality between men and between women (also called lesbianism) Homosexuality is very serious sin. God judged these cities in part because the homosexuals did not hide their sin.

> *"..And they display their sin like Sodom; they do not even conceal it. Woe to them! For they have brought evil on themselves." (Isa. 3:9)*

> *"And Lot, when he said to his people, "Do you commit an obscenity not perpetrated before you by anyone in all the worlds? You come with lust to men instead of women. You are indeed a depraved people." (Qur'an, 7:80-81)*

> *"..and if He condemned the cities of Sodom and Gomorrah to destruction by reducing them to ashes, having made them an example to those who would live ungodly thereafter..." (2 Peter 2:6)*

> *"*Our Messengers said to Lot,+ "We will bring down on the inhabitants of this city a devastating punishment from heaven because of their deviance." We have left a Clear Sign of them behind for people who use their intellect." (Qur'an, 29:34-35)*

Conclusion: A Mighty God predicted Sodom and Gomorrah would never be inhabited again. [Jer 49:18] *"Like the overthrow of Sodom and Gomorrah with its neighbors," says the LORD, "no one will live there, nor will a son of man reside in it.* The above prophecy was fair and just and we can see ancient Sodom and Gomorrah does not exist today. Think this over. Around the time, 4,100 years ago, when ancient Sodom and Gomorrah was destroyed, ancient China, ancient India, ancient Vietnam, and ancient Egypt (Khem) were thriving. So these nations continued to exist even in the fog of the divine destruction of the most depraved people/government on earth, *Sodom and Gomorrah,* at that time. As the old adage says: "one monkey don't stop no show."

17. How has the leadership of the Caucasian race failed to conduct good government over the past 600 years since conquering the Americas?

___
___
___
___
___
___
___
___
___
___
___
___
___
___
___
___
___
___
___
___

SIX

The Constitution

All governments necessitate some form of a constitution to gain Consent of the Governed and backing of its citizens. Or at least that is the objective. For instance, in 1972 the Honorable Elijah Muhammad fielded questions by the Black Press regarding this issue. Near the end of the interview, the following questions and answers hit the mark.

> ~~Question:~~ How will your resources be administered?
> ~~Messenger:~~ That will be carried on by the Nation. After setting up the Nation on the right way, or right path, to take care of themselves, they do not need any more instruction on that. They will follow it as the Constitution of America has been followed.
> ~~Question:~~ Will it be run by local Mosques?
> ~~Messenger:~~ No, No, No. After this, the whole entire Nation of Black people will be governed divinely and the government will be a Divine government and not something that is governed locally, like we have today. We will have a Divine government set up for us, and it will stand forever. We will not need any change.
> ~~Question:~~ What did you mean, "new, different from Orthodox?"
> ~~Messenger:~~ I meant just that. We have a New Islam coming up. The Old Islam was led by white people, white Muslims, but this one will not be. This Islam will

be established and led by Black Muslims, only.[29]

Governments are only justified and legal when derived from the people or society over which that political power is exercised. This theory of "consent" is historically contrasted to the divine right of kings and has often been invoked against the legitimacy of colonialism. [10] There are no kingship rulers in Islam.

As for the Nation of Islam of the West, it has gained consent of its members because they are rooted in love thy brother/sister as thyself; and has functioned as such since July 4, 1930 by Allah's grace and mercy. And thanks to the ancient world of Islam for leaving a blue print that allows one to see how good government structure is able to generate success to unite people of many different cultures, folkways and morays. By this we mean a little known fact regarding Consent of the governed was demonstrated by the first Islamic government constitution written by the last Islamic prophet of Arabia, Mohammed Ibn Abdullah. He drafted what is called the **Constitution of Medina** over 1,400 years ago. It was employed to unite.

"The Constitution of Medina (Arabic: " # $ &(+ * ,-, Ṣaḥīfat al-Madīnah), also known as the Charter of Medina, was drafted by the Islamic prophet Muhammad. It **constituted a formal agreement between Muhammad and all of the significant tribes and families of Yathrib** (later known as Medina), including **Muslims, Jews, Christians and pagans.** This constitution formed the basis of the future caliphate. **The document was drawn up with the explicit concern of bringing to an end the bitter inter tribal fighting between the clans of the Aws (Aus) and Khazraj within Medina.** To this effect it instituted a number of rights and responsibilities for the Muslim, Jewish, Christian and pagan communities of Medina bringing them within the fold of one

---

[29] Muhammad Speaks Newspaper February 4, 1972

community—the Ummah.

"The precise dating of the Constitution of Medina remains debated but generally scholars agree it was written shortly after the Hijra (622). **It effectively established the first Islamic state.** The Constitution established: the security of the community, religious freedoms, the role of Medina as a haram or sacred place (barring all violence and weapons), the security of women, stable tribal relations within Medina, a tax system for supporting the community in time of conflict, parameters for exogenous political alliances, a system for granting protection of individuals, a judicial system for resolving disputes, and also regulated the paying of blood money (the payment between families or tribes for the slaying of an individual in lieu of lex talionis). [11]

We know the United States Constitution did not formerly include the rights of aboriginal Black, Brown and Red people 237 years ago. Even to this day America is slow-walking how to transition from her old ways into a new reality she now faces. "White" isn't what it used to be.

On the other hand, the Medina Constitution included all people, 1,400 years ago, for the sake of life, liberty and the pursuit of happiness. Prophet Mohammed knew what reality Islam faced and what each tribe was facing as well. He desired peace and not war to avoid oppression of one tribe over another. All agreed with his plan except to enemy of freedom.

18. Who wrote the U.S. Constitution and what is the purpose of a constitution?

_____
_____
_____
_____
_____

In terms of the Medina Constitution, although merely rehearsed 1,400 years ago by people of past times, can Black America thinks to use its principles to unite and transition into a righteous nation structure? And if not, why not? Have not you witnessed how over the past 80 plus years, Nation of Islam Laborers has marked the greatest experience of unity and transitional structure by **Allah's authority** than any other African American operation? Can you recognize how the NOI is setting a process in motion to unite our tribes and/or Black families, be they Muslims, Black Jews, Black Christians and modern day pagans (those who reject God theology) from every hood and prison?

The NOI's 80 plus years represent the greatest forward-work in spite being constantly opposed by many enemies dating back to Jim Crow of 1877 to the US Gov. against Black Wall Street of 1921 to FBI agents sabotaging Whiting H&G of 1975.

9 Ministries

During Saviours' Day 2006, themed "The Birth of a Nation," the Honorable Minister Louis Farrakhan hosted presenters to set forth an overview of the Nine Ministries to expand NOI business functions as good as a government should operate. What is a ministry?

"A ministry is a specialized organization responsible for a sector of government public administration, sometimes led by a minister or a senior public servant, that can have responsibility for one or more departments, agencies, bureaus, commissions or other smaller executive, advisory, managerial or administrative organizations.

"Ministries are usually subordinate to the cabinet, and prime minister, president or chancellor.

"A government will usually have numerous ministries, each with a specialized field of providing public service. National ministries vary greatly between countries, but some common ones include Ministry of Defense, Ministry of Foreign Affairs, Ministry of Finance, and Ministry of Health." [12]

Of course, ministries exist in many nations of the earth. For example, Jamaica, Barbados and Grenada all have Ministry Departments.

But no current nation or leader on earth has received what the scriptures predicted in [1 Corinthians 2:9]. Only a small percent of the people believe this ultimate reality has been reserved for those whom Allah—the Divine Supreme Being has come to free from mental death under *"white authority"* to transition into the best part of the hereafter. Believe you me, the best part of the hereafter will not be inside Iron Mountain due to special US government qualifications and credentials.

For now nine ministries possibly will be employed, today, by Black America, to transition from where we are into a new reality toward government structure and nationhood. Talk about special...these nine ministries should be seen as offices to perform services. Yes, services because any man or women working in a government capacity are servants of its citizenry to ensure freedom, justice, equality, money, good homes, etc, for the citizen.

By the thousands Muslims are being qualified for positions awaiting them.

For instance, all NOI ministries function under the

Executive Branch of the Nation of Islam. Its Executive Branch is the central key to maintain all necessary structural transitions. Today the (9) ministries are being established by Laborers (servants) who understand and believe in the everlasting principles of Islam (peace). This ongoing expansion being exemplified by the NOI is merely an example of what Black America must do towards making great progress in establishing a new and better environment for life, a more abundant life.

Charlene Muhammad, a final call correspondent, wrote on March 7, 2006: "the ministries were drawn out of a conversation with Minister Farrakhan regarding the future of the N.O.I..". The following 9 fields of Ministries necessitate:

Health & Human Services
Agriculture
Education
Defense
Art & Culture
Trade & Commerce
Justice
Information
Science & Technology

What is a **Ministry of Health and Human Services**? To begin with, the basics of **Health and Human ministry**, is to protect the health of all citizens of a nation and providing essential human services.

Human services refer to a variety of delivery systems such as social welfare services, education, mental health services, and other forms of healthcare. This area of government must have qualified professionals to ensure successful progress and outcomes.

The M.G.T. & G.C.C.: I can sit on top of the world and tell everyone that the most beautiful Nation is in the wilderness of North America.

But do not let me catch any sister other than herself in regards to living the Life and weighing properly.[13]

Dr. Abdul Alim Muhammad is Minister of Health and Human Services of the Nation of Islam. He is a minister and surgeon who has held several teaching positions at various medical centers and universities. In 1986, he founded the Abundant Life Clinic in Washington, D.C., which enabled him to pursue community-based alternative medicine. He is known around the world for his clinical research in HIV/AIDS.[30]

Next is what a **Ministry of Agriculture**? Its basic aim is to meet the needs of farmers and ranchers, promote agricultural trade and production, work to assure food safety and protect natural resources.

The student must study his Assignment--Lesson #1.
Each Student should copy the Answers of Lesson of Minister, Elijah Muhammad, and study until the Student is able to memorize, By Heart, all Answers to, of said, Lesson #1.

NOTE: Here, Lesson #1 is said to be the Student's Assignment-"First." LESSON #1 lays the Base of our Work today; and gives the Student a Clear Knowledge of Himself and His Heavenly Home, the Best Part of the Earth; and who is the enemy to him and his Nation; and why the enemy and Righteous could not live together; and why was the Righteous able to Cast Out his enemy. [14]

---

[30] Google: Askia Muhammad in a brief one-on-one interview with Dr. Abdul Alim Muhammad.

THIS Teaches the student what he must do with the enemy of the Righteous today. THE Righteous Nation is, now, Living in every part of the planet Earth. Therefore the enemy must, now, be removed in every part of the planet Earth...[15]

What is a **Ministry of Education**? Its basic mission is to promote student achievement and preparation for global competitiveness by fostering educational excellence and the knowledge of government and civics. In addition, it functions to establish policy to, administer and coordinate all level school systems for and colleges with a centralized curricula or educational standards.

The TEMPLE READING CLASS: The Reading Class shall include all of the History. Report the Reading Class along with the regular School Report.

The Secretary must report once a week of the Educational Department and a general report of the Temple. [16]

In the United States school system one problem has been keeping too many people under-educated, especially with respect to how citizens are to relate to their government and how government servants are to relate to its citizenry. Is it by accident that so much opposition has been hatched against a school curriculum to educate U.S. citizens into the knowledge of government, structure and civics?

For example, the following portion is a small part of a curricula of said subject that has been opposed in Delaware:

"This curriculum framework rests on the foundation of four core disciplines from the social sciences: history, geography, economics, and civics. Each discipline offers a distinct strategy for examining the world, and provides students with specific intellectual and conceptual tools for analyzing causes and consequences. A more extensive list of subjects could be suggested, and it is encouraging when any district dedicates the time and resources to expanding this framework beyond the core disciplines. Nothing in this document is intended to discourage such initiatives. We do believe, however, that history, geography, economics, and civics are the essential focus for citizenship education, and that their importance should not be diminished."

Therefore, by the thousands God is preparing and qualifying men and women for positions awaiting them for His Universal Government of Peace.

What is a **Ministry of Defense**? It's a Department who's primarily concerned is ensuring the secure and stable environment necessary for economic growth and development. In the Nation of Islam, our Executive Department of Government, under the Supreme Captain of the NOI, is charged with coordinating and supervising all agencies and functions of the elements concerned directly with national security. **Ministry of Defense** is also very critical for maintaining public safety and business growth. Can Black America learn much from the inner workings of how to improve our community's immediate environment by understanding defense?

19. What is defense?
_____
_____
_____
_____
_____
_____
_____

20. What is offense?
_____
_____

Over the past 6,600 years, this current world order was given to the practice of murder and lying. Such evil practice was initiated by a group of the most dissatisfied and problematic Black men and women over 6,600 years ago on the Greek Isles of Patmos. Consequently, from this group were produced members of the so-called white race 6,000 years ago. In genetic terms, these people were made genetically recessive ("aa" trait), which represents an opposite in genetic dominance.

Members of the Original Black nation are carriers of the "AA" (dominate trait) and/or "Aa" *incomplete dominance* genetic trait. So hidden within the genetic creative nature of the Black nation, is a recessive *incomplete dominant trait or marker*. I suggest you read, "Message To The Blackman" by Elijah Muhammad to full grasp what occurred on the islands of Patmos (Pelan).

In effect, the Original Black nation had no defense to prevent the making of an entire genetically recessive "aa" gene carrier—the so-called white race. Nevertheless, today their rule is ending, but they are making war to continue exercising their rule. These men of war that are on the offensive, militarily, until after a massive war—WWIII.

Will the NOI **Ministry of Defense** be the largest employer due to the evil practices learned by Black people since living directly under the influence of an old wicked order of white authority? Is not public safety the highest standard of any civilized society? Will Black America respond to righteous law or do we know what righteous law represents without argument from ignorance? How and why is peace secured by strength? Can we accept simple standards between right and wrong conduct?

Application For Enlistment in the Fruit of Islam will be accepted on the Approval of their Holy Names. Names of Devils are not counted of any value in the Fruit of Islam.

Devils must stay away. [17]

    21. What is an incomplete dominance trait and where does it exist?

_____
_____
_____
_____
_____
_____

Universal War Before Universal Government of Peace

    Allah (God) is acknowledged as the sole sovereign of human affairs and has always intervened into human affairs. God raised prophets and prophetess to secure the spiritual and materials needs [needed] for the people denied to which government officials were to implement.

    In 1935, on July 31st, the Honorable Elijah Muhammad wrote to his ministers of Islam and said:

"My Dear Ministers, we follow no more the old world of wickedness and blindness, of greed and lust and hate and jealousy which are sins that causes brotherly love to wax cold toward one another; therefore, we can give freely out of love the blessings we receive from Him without envy, because this is the Fundamental Principle of a Moslem's faith, is to love his brother as his ownself and give out of Allah's right course to thou Allah; and these are the successful ones...[31]

When citizens have good government and management, people have a guarantee of societal rights in all areas of education and economics in spite stratification disadvantages—*the way in which different groups of people are placed within society; mainly based upon money or the lack thereof*—*and an assortment of other mental or chemical deficiencies.*

As a result, during these end times; Allah (God) in Person appeared Himself in the West to intervene into the affairs of America's former slaves according to what past prophets predicted. [Genesis 15:14; Deuteronomy 18:18]. This Divine Being, Allah, as mentioned earlier in this book was once tracked by the U.S. Federal Government. But why? Was it because He was a Ghost? Or was it because Allah's ultimate goal is to bring about a universal government of peace? Is it because He chose the Lost and Found people of America to lead such a kingdom? Or is it because an Islamic kingdom is rooted in two basic axes: (1) law and legislation, and (2) management and implementation of divine law? No matter what reason, no one can stop Allah's will and purpose! For if God be with us, who can be against us! [Romans 8:31]

During the 1950's, another Nation of Islam pioneer registered to help establish what he defined as the Kingdom of God. His name is Don Muhammad. He is the minster of Muhammad Mosque 11, Boston, Massachusetts. During a pbs.org interview, he states his beliefs and recalls:

---

[31] Ministry Class Taught By The Most Hon. Elijah Muhammad Vol. 2

"Minister Farrakhan was speaking. His subject was Who is God, what is He, and where is He? He talked that day for nearly 5 hours on the reality of God. And that message that day helped me to confirm that there is a God that He is very interested in the affairs of human beings, and **I was further able to see the intervention of God in establishing His Kingdom. And that is why I decided to join the Nation of Islam.**"[32]

Once again, will there really be a universal war before any universal government can be established before He (Allah) brings about a universal government of peace wherein we all can live in peace together.

"The Most Honorable Elijah Muhammad also explained to many of his followers that we would experience a period where the sun will not give her light for several days driving many people to near insanity. The entire cosmos, the sun, the moon and the stars and other objects in space will be used as the weapons of God threatening the entire life on our planet in this time of Universal War. The work of the angels described by the Most Honorable Elijah Muhammad is not coming from invisible or unseen beings. These angels are born and are highly trained in their work and mission from early childhood. In a similar way to that of the Great Mahdi Himself, Master W. F. Muhammad, who was prepared for his mission by his father since he was a little boy. The power of God and the scientists of the angelic hosts work with telepathic knowledge and advanced technologies that are far beyond the Knowledge of this world. They have mastered super consciousness in their being that are not to be played with. They are prepared to deliver the righteous taking them across these turbulent waters of the present global crises safely to the other side.

"To our readers, never doubt any of the Divine Messages and

---

[32] www.pbs.org/thisfarbyfaith/transcript/**minister_don_muhammad**.pdf

Teachings of the Most Honorable Elijah Muhammad or those of his greatest Helper and Warner in our midst today, the Honorable Minister Louis Farrakhan. Listen to the small, still voice within and follow the instructions that we are being given in this time of the fall and destruction of an entire world of Satan's dominion. In one of our Supreme Wisdom Lessons, Problem Number 31, we are told not to lose time, to ask questions and learn all about yourself. "What are you doing today for yourself? Your Brother from the East wants to know and hear from you at once!"[33]

---

[33] http://www.finalcall.com/artman/publish/Columns_4/article_9379.shtml

SEVEN

Basic Government Structure

Western civilization owes its very existence to all highly developed ancient Black civilizations from ancient Bekkah, Sumer, India, China and Khemet (Egypt). It was our wise forefathers' who taught government structural knowledge and mathematics to the Gogs and Magogs. In addition, were it not for the ancient Islamic world influence, Europe would have remained in the dark ages under Papal rule yet teaching its masses that the earth is flat.

With that being said, let us look at some ideas of limited government, rule of law, Democracy and representative government. These concepts were originally designed to enable government Laborers to serve (not rule) over the masses of people.

Limited government—In a **limited government**, the power of government to intervene in the exercise of civil liberties is restricted by law, usually in a written constitution. The theory of limited government contrasts, for example, with the ideal that government should intervene to promote equality and opportunity through regulation of property and wealth redistribution.

Rule of law—The *rule of law* means everyone must obey the law, including citizens, non-citizens, and government leaders.
The police and the courts enforce the laws.
The police and the courts must also obey the laws.

Democracy—Several variants of democracy exist, but there are two basic forms, both of which concern how the whole body of citizens executes its will. One form of democracy is direct democracy, in which citizens have an active participation in the decision making of the government. In most modern democracies, the whole body of citizens remains the sovereign power but political power is exercised indirectly through elected representatives; this is called representative democracy.

On the subject of democracy, "How to protect a democracy", Minister Louis Farrakhan stated on August 2004, Final Call Newspaper:

"Democracy, which is the highest form of government that we know at this time, presupposes an enlightened electorate where you, the electors of those whom you will elect, have knowledge of what is in your best interest. Democracy presupposes that you are so enlightened, so intelligent, that you do not choose a candidate because he or she has a slick ad on television. The question for the candidate becomes, what do you propose that fits what I believe is good for my neighborhood, my ward, my city, my state, my nation?

"But, how can democracy be saved when the electorate is being absolutely dumbed down—dumbing down the children, dumbing down the electorate? Corporate America is taking over newspapers, radio and television and managing what you see and what you hear. Corporate America is controlling how you think. The human masses have become like sheep—easily led in the wrong direction.

"Why am I saying this? It is because the country is being taken from the people. The country is owned lock, stock and barrel by a few, to the detriment of the many. That's why there is such a thing as campaign finance reform; it is because corporate America spends billions of dollars buying the votes of those who have been elected to serve the people."

Representative government—People chosen by the citizens of the land to make decisions on their behalf and to represent them in the legislative assembly.

The provisional constitution of the Nation of Islam, under the leadership of Minister Louis Farrakhan Muhammad, and its executive council, at its heart, involve all registered NOI members in what Allah (God) has promised that is - luxury, money, good homes, friendship in all walks of life. [18] In turn, one transition after the next, such life resources shall be shared with all humanity. This life to come while we live is a way of life western civilization has ruined for all humanity due to its greedy and wasteful nature!

In 1935, on July 31 the Honorable Elijah Muhammad laid a base for the mindset of his ministers to love enough to produce said above transition into a much better life. He wrote:

"Remember brothers, how we were taught by the devil's representatives, who are the preachers, to seek one's own good and his brother could starve him and his family; but let us as Ministers of the New Kingdom of Freedom, Justice and Equality which our Righteous Savior, the Mighty Allah is setting up, and has chosen us Ministers as of its foundation stone, and Light Bearers of Him…"[34]

The above memo speaks to the **10th Ministry of the Nation of Islam**—its spiritual department.

You might ask: Is a full constitution being prepared for members of the Nation of Islam for governmental purposes? And if so, how will luxury, money, good homes, friendship in all walks of life be accomplished for all? First, with the best and neatest workers, second, by men and women that understands his or her civic duty, and third by the active will of The All Mighty Allah!

Thus the reason all political, spiritual and educational activity of the NOI is always disseminated from Muhammad Mosques of Islam or other NOI electronic official networks.

---

[34] Ministry Class Taught By The Most Honorable Elijah Muhammad Vol. 1.

Brothers and Sisters, you all get busy and help to Arise the dead Nation, and place them on top of civilization. My dearest Desire is to give everyone his or her own.

I do not want importance among the Officials nor the Laborers.
Do not do other than yourself.

Do not take on Mixed Instructions other than OUR ASSIGNMENT. [19]

What is a **Ministry of Justice?** It is responsible for the enforcement of the law and administration of justice—a "law department". The Honorable Elijah Muhammad said *"justice is the reward of good and punishment for evil"*. Of course, the law department of a universal government need not be as expansive as the old wicked world order, which thrives on corruption and profits on corruption. Investigations into great crimes are even corrupted.

Absence in the Ministers' Class must always be investigated. [20]

Each ministry needed to establish and expand the NOI structure here and now was contoured by Master W. Fard Muhammad, the Divine Supreme Being, during his three and one-half year ministry with the Honorable Elijah Muhammad.

In terms of the law of Justice to govern registered NOI members, the Honorable Minister Louis Farrakhan has completed a law book of 26 restrictive laws entitled, "**The Restrictive Laws of Islam Is Our Success**." These laws were originally prepared by Master W. Fard Muhammad and represent the essential divine laws written in Bible and Quran to correct personal and social misbehavior: *"a Law that demands...constant attention"*. Perhaps then we may live a better way of life while we live.

As it was once related by minister Jabril Muhammad,

the Honorable Elijah stated even though we (Black Muslims) will rule inside of North America for 20 years, there will be some who will yet practice evil (breaking laws of Islam) in secret?

Think about underground drug dealing, alcoholic usage, prostitution, public indecent exposure, child molestation, adultery, fornication, surreptitious after hour clubs in basement of homes, and other rotten filth that some may feel they have a right to practice. Under white authority, such acts are practiced daily. How long should these practices continue? Are these practices taking place today, in secret venues, in the Holy Land?

While the ruling elite heel to the footsteps of Satan's Golden Calf by worshiping wealth, thousands of students are Qualifying self for Positions awaiting them to work for Allah!

<u>Each Student must qualify his or herself for Positions awaiting them. Assignment of Office will be made immediately after Examination, and on Completion of his or her Labor Course.</u>

<u>Consideration for the Laborers of Islam will be taken, and Analysis, in the near future by ALLAH!</u>

<u>NOTE: THIS PARAGRAPH puts a stop to all Quarreling and Arguments among the Laborers over their Offices in ISLAM until he or she have been qualified and their qualification Examined to see if they are Fit to be used in the Respective Position.</u>

<u>THE past History shows that the First Examination of Laborers is made by the Apostle, whom the Laborers are to work with.</u> [21]

The Honorable Elijah Muhammad said "the righteous members of the Nation of Islam, we will be Changed into a New and Perfect People; and Fill the Earth with FREEDOM, JUSTICE and EQUALITY as it was filled with wickedness, and Making we, the Poor Lost-Founds, the Perfect RULERS."

It's no wonder why Laborers of the NOI desire to pass the final examination before entering into what no eye has seen or ear has heard, nor has it entered into the hearts of men. [1 Corinthians 2:9-10] *"But as it is written, Eye has not seen, nor ear heard, neither have entered into the heart of man, the things which God has prepared for them that love him. These are the things God has revealed to us by his Spirit. The Spirit searches all things, even the deep things of God."*

There is a universal transition going on now to bring about the NEW! *(See Appendix 3, Six Thousand Year Transition of Nations pg. 169)* The best part of the Hereafter, according to the teachings of the Hon. Elijah Muhammad, is while we live, not after physical death.

22. What is the meaning of "Restrictive Law"?

_____
_____
_____
_____

Do you think one reason members of the Nation of Islam are destined to become the greatest nation on earth is that "We" all speak the same language. Yet free to use our own dialect.

"The term dialect (from the ancient Greek word Διάλεκτος *diálektos*, "discourse", from διά *diá*, "through" + λζγω *legō*, "I speak") is used in two distinct ways, even by linguists. One usage refers to a variety of a language that is a characteristic of a particular group of the language's speakers. The term is applied most often to regional speech patterns, but a dialect may also be defined by other factors, such as social class." [22]

Knowledge about dialect is contained within the Supreme Wisdom Book of the Nation of Islam. We were given specific instructions about the importance of proper language usage. It reads in part:

Why should the Lost-Founds Disbelieve and Dispute with one another about OUR SAVIOUR (ALLAH) and HIS Work of Delivering? Cannot a Fool see that a Mighty Change is in Progress in every Living Creature?

The Laborers must practice the above Language with all new Converts.

The Laborers are liable to punishment if found using Baby Language at any time.

The Laborers must greet a Registered Muslim in his own way. [23]

In the Nation of Islam, there are no democrats, republicans, libertarians, Sunni, Shia and what not's. There are only Muslim brothers and sisters. Isn't that how Allah planned it? Not difficult to understand is it?

EIGHT

Ministry of Finance

Finance is a matter of applying mathematics correctly. Whether finances of nations or personal business, a financial statement demonstrates value or undervalue.

"A financial statement that lists the assets, liabilities and equity of a company at a specific point in time and is used to calculate the net worth of a business. A basic tenet of double-entry bookkeeping is that total assets (what a business owns) must equal liabilities plus equity (how the assets are financed). In other words, the balance sheet must balance. Subtracting liabilities from assets shows the net worth of the business A basic tenet of double-entry bookkeeping is that total assets (what a business owns) must equal liabilities plus equity (how the assets are financed). In other words, the balance sheet must balance."[35]

In business contracts and government accounting, it's a matter of honest ratio management and calculation to avoid corruption, lying, cheating, profiteering and stealing and corrupt double book accounting. Good finance must be about recycling currency for continuous wealth distribution from city to city, state to state, business to business, government to government for the good of its citizenry!

After learning Mathematics, which is Islam, and Islam is Mathematics, it stands true. You can always prove it at no limit of time. Then you must learn to use it and secure some benefit while you are living, that is - luxury, money, good homes, friendship in all walks of life.

Sit yourself in Heaven at once! That is the greatest Desire of your

---

[35] http://www.entrepreneur.com/encyclopedia/term/82186.html#

Brother and Teachers.

Now you must speak the Language so you can use your Mathematical Theology in the proper Term-otherwise you will not be successful unless you do speak well, for she knows all about you.

The Secretary of Islam offers a reward to the best and neatest worker of this Problem. [24]

    Will good finance materialize under a New World of Islam, wherein no one will be taxed in the manner we have been under white authority?
    Islam teaches charity purifies the heart.

"In Islam, taxation is called **Zakāt (Arabic:** !"[zæˈ kæ,] "that which purifies", is the giving of a fixed portion of one's wealth as a tax, generally to the poor.

"The amount of zakat to be paid on capital assets (e.g. money) is 2.5% (1/40). Zakat is additionally payable on agricultural goods, precious metals, minerals, and livestock at a rate varying between 2.5 (1/40) and 20 percent, depending on the type of goods."

    What are assets? Assets represent the materials used to make money (profits) as opposed to assets used for personal enjoyment or consumption. Assets are a resource with economic value that an individual, corporation or country owns or controls with the expectation that it will provide future benefit. Therefore, the greatest asset promised to members of the Lost and Founds of North America is land, mineral rich land! This is what the Jews wanted and land is what the white Christians wanted. So why expect less for America's descendants of former slaves.

    23. What is the difference between charity and taxation?
_____
_____

An Islamic miracle is unfolding inside North America. As stated before, no taxation will be required in the New world of Islam. **Without a private owned central bank siphoning off the wealth of a nation, there would be no need for a personal income tax.**

So what is a **Ministry of Trade and Commerce?** It is a job creation operation for economic growth, sustainable development and improved standards of living for all citizens of a nation. The **ministry of finance** works in partnership with local businesses, universities, communities and a nation's workers in general.

24. What is the meaning of economic value?

A **Ministry of Finance** department touches the daily lives of the people in many ways, with a wide range of responsibilities in the areas of trade, economic development and technical assistance to its citizens, entrepreneurship and business development. In addition, statistical research and analysis of successful business incubators is good for citizens that might invest their hard earned income to earn profits from well established business models.

Imagine being part owner of the goods and services of everything you purchase to recycle your income back into your account. Imagine a universal stock market structure designed, monitored and governed by the righteous to keep wealth on main street. Suggested reading for insight into these matters is a book entitled, *Torchlight For America"* by Minister Louis Farrakhan.

Overall, Black America has enough educated men and women to operate as good as their own nation and engage in international trade and commerce with other nations. And soon enough, those whom have been force-tied promoting white lies and policies shall be given permission, one day, to help Elijah Muhammad and his Minister Louis Farrakhan so it is written. [Quran 20:70-73]

"70. The wizard were (all) flung down prostrate, crying: We believe in the Lord of Aaron and Moses. 71. (Pharaoh) said: Ye put faith in him before I give you permission (leave). Lo! He is your chief who taught you magic. Now surely I shall cut off your hands and your feet alternately and I shall crucify you on the trucks of palm trees, and ye shall know for certain which of us has sterner and more lasting punishment. 72. They said: We choose thee not above the clear proofs that have come unto us, and above Him Who created us. So decree what thou wilt decree. Thou wilt end for us this life of the world. 73. Lo! We believe in our Lord, that He may forgive us our sins and the magic

unto which thou didst force us. Allah is better and more lasting..."

Political System of Old World Islam

Why and how did the old world Muslim community become side-tracked politically speaking?

"Owing to the dominant perception among Islamic political thinkers that the umma **(MUSLIM COMMUNITY)** was the basic collective religio-political unit, the concept of the state was not well delineated until Ibn Khaldun articulated his idea of the state in the 14th century. He did not conceive the idea of "state" in the sense that it was devised by the Romans and later reframed in Europe. Rather, Ibn Khaldun set forth the notion of the umma as **(MUSLIM COMMUNITY)** a distinctive Muslim polity. In this context, it must be recalled that the umma **(MUSLIM COMMUNITY)** extended to wherever there were Muslims whatever the prevailing conditions and ideology…the umma **(MUSLIM COMMUNITY)** - reinforced by the morally delineated role of government in Islamic society - was the hallmark distinction between Islamic political thought and that of the Christian successors of the Roman Empire who never divorced themselves from the Roman idea of a territorially defined organization of power. Muslims, until modern times, identified themselves primarily as members of the Islamic community locally and generally, wherever it existed. Until the advent of 19th and 20th century nationalism together with various degrees of secularism in the Muslim world, the idea of an Islamic state in the Western sense remained largely **un-crystalized** in Muslim thought."[36]

For instance, GHULAM SARWAR--Director of the Muslim Educational Trust propounds, "Religion and politics are one and the same in Islam. They are intertwined. We already know that Islam is a complete system of life and politics is very much a part of our collective life…Bear in mind that Islamic ruling system is not the same as the ruling system we have in the non-Islamic countries.

---
[36] http://www.upenn.edu/emeritus/events/IslamConcepts.pdf

"The duty of an Islamic state is to establish Salah and Zakah; promote the right and forbid the wrong (22:44). The state is responsible for the welfare of all its citizens - Muslims and non-Muslims alike. It must guarantee the basic necessities of life. All citizens of the Islamic state shall enjoy freedom of belief, thought, conscience and speech. Every citizen shall be free to develop his potential, improve his capacity, earn and possess. A citizen shall enjoy the right to support or oppose any government policy which he thinks right or wrong with the following in mind.

"The Islamic state is a duty bound to implement the laws of the Qur'an and the Sunnah. The Qur'an strongly denounces those who do not decide their matters by Allah's revelations (5:42-50).

"The Islamic state shall ensure a fair distribution of wealth. Islam does not believe in equal distribution as it is against the law of creation.

"There is not a single perfect Islamic state in the world today. There are many Muslim countries. An Islamic state is based on the model of Prophet Muhammad's (phuh) state in Madinah while a Muslim state is one which has a majority Muslim population and some Islamic features.

"However, organized efforts have been going on in many Muslim countries to establish truly Islamic states. Al-ikhwanul Muslimun in the Middle East, Muzahid or Taliban in Afganistan, the Jama'at-e-Islami in Pakistan, and Kashmir, Jehaad movement in Bangladesh, Dewan Dakwah Islamia (Islamic Dawah Council) in Indonesia, Al-Muhajirun in Britain, and Hizb-ut-Tahrir in most advanced Islamic (Muslim population) countries are some of the Islamic movements and parties which have been working for the re-establishment of Allah's law on Allah's land."

But what Ghulam Sarwar does not mention is the Nation of Islam in the West. The question is why not? Answer: It is neither his mission nor job. The **NOI's success** is being established from top, to middle, to bottom by the Divine Active will of Allah. Not with the weaponry of the western world produced by the so-called white man. **Allah's weapons are every force of nature in the heavens above to the earth beneath, including shooting stars.**

Rightly so, a New world of Islam (Kingdom of Peace) is being established regardless as to who likes it or not! Allah is now giving it over to the Lost and Found members of the Black Nation of the West that will square the nations of the earth. Take it, you cannot let it alone!

On December 22, 1967 the Honorable Elijah Muhammad wrote in the Muhammad Speaks Newspaper the following:

"TODAY, God, in the Person of Master Fard Muhammad, has revealed this truth and has opened their eyes to more knowledge than they ever knew. This knowledge is given to a people just prior to their destruction. He allows them to take a peek into the Knowledge of God and His power so that they will not make the mistake of trying to attack the Creator, which will be a losing battle.

"The white race-especially America-ruling over the Black people (her slaves, the so-called Negroes), beating and killing them day and night, corresponds with a savage beast. What is causing a divine judgment of justice to come upon America is her cruel and evil treatment of her slave, the so-called America Negro, to whom she has never, according to her history, shown mercy and leniency in giving them freedom, justice and equality or giving them an equal chance to qualify themselves as equals with other civilized nations of the earth, to win the love and respect of their own people.

"BUT, EVIL could not capture us 100 per cent, within 6000 years, due to the Mahdi (Messiah) being born at the end of 6,000 years from the birth of Yakub (the father of the white race), whose wisdom was limited to the birth and coming of the Great Mahdi, God in Person, (of the righteous).

"The coming of the Mahdi as being One greater in knowledge and greater in wisdom than Yakub was seen and prophesied by Yakub and he prophesied His coming after him to destroy his civilization in Revelation.

"IT IS mentioned that he saw One coming after him Whose brightness (wisdom) of His coming would destroy his made man and his made man's wisdom (the white race), for it is superior wisdom that rules the people.

"The world of the white race is angry because of the superior wisdom of the Mahdi that is being taught to the inferior — especially the America so-called Negroes. It is angering them and finally will cause a complete vanishing of the wisdom of the white race which has rule Black people like a savage beast and which now tries to deceive those who are yet asleep to the knowledge of the white race by showing false friendship, false promises of wealth, and high positions in his government.

"BEING ignorant of such teachings coming from the slave master's children will cause the destruction of hundreds of thousands and maybe millions of so-called American Negroes seeking temporary enjoyment of life from their enemies.

"They will get all of this permanently from the Great Mahdi (Master Fard Muhammad) who will fulfill His promise to us if we believe. He promised heaven at once to the Negro believers."

Can the U.S. Government provide jobs to her own unemployed let along 40 to 60 million Black people? Will America function as a Welfare State beyond 2017? *(See Appendix 4: U.S. Debt August 15, 2021 12:07 PM pg. 174)*

NINE

Ministry of Information

This particular department of information is now transitioning to expand. Year 2014 will be 80 years from the time, 1934; Mr. Elijah Muhammad's Teacher imparted to him the knowledge of the time; how and why Black people were brought in slavery, the enemy who committed such crime and what great blessing is to come as result of our suffering.

But imagine in general, if America's slaves and former slaves would have retained their history from the beginning of U.S. slavery. The International Representative of the NOI, Akbar Muhammad, has stated:

"Imagine if the slaves were free to pass on their oral history to the generations from 1555 to 2010—455 years. We would still have a sense of our language, culture, religion and an idea of where we came from on the African continent. This oral history would have informed us of our names when we arrived in America. This oral history would identify the names and places of the plantations and of the slave masters. There would have been stories repeated over and over again about the ships that brought us here and what happened on those ships. This oral history would have helped us keep contact with our family members.

"Most of us know that we were deprived of learning how to read and write. The elders would have taken the young and repeated these stories to them, which would have also helped us, retain words from our own languages.

"Instead what we have are remnants, oral histories of former slaves and their descendants that were recorded in the 1930s as part of the New Deal-era Works Progress Administration (WPA). During the Great Depression, as part of the federal government's massive employment program, millions were employed to complete public works projects, including programs in the arts, literacy, and historical preservation. These WPA narratives and what could be remembered by the children and the adults forms the basis of a complete reevaluation of the history of slavery. One of the most interesting aspects of the story told by the former slaves and their children was recalling the Muslim practices of their ancestors and parents.

"It was the Black historian John Blassingame, who in 1972 challenged the account of slavery given by the slave-owner/masters. In his book, "The Slave Community; Plantation life in the Antebellum South," Mr. Blassingame presented the slave as the agent of his own history. In the Nation of Islam today, Carlos Muhammad, one of Minister Farrakhan's young representatives from Baltimore has committed to pull together the history of the NOI, not from the eyes of outsiders, but from the voices and deeds of those who lived that history themselves."[37]

Any government **Ministry of Information** aims to provide the public with up-to-date, comprehensive and meaningful information with government policies, services and activities as well as on matters of public interest. The main function of the ministry of Information is to provide a link between the Government and the public and provides the following services:

Electronic Services
The department manages the Government Portal, the Intranet for the Public Service and official pages on social media networks and other events of national importance is produced by the department and electronically dispatched to overseas Diplomatic Missions and Consulates.

---

[37] http://www.finalcall.com/artman/publish/Perspectives_1/article_6726.shtml

Government Information Service

The Government Information Service provides members of the general public with information and material relevant to Government services and activities. The Government Information Service is available by means of e-mail. The Government Information Service welcomes members of the public who call in person at its Customer Care Office to obtain information.

Media Monitoring Unit

The section monitors the most recent political, economic and social development issues, reported in the local print media.

Media Relations

Media organizations are daily supplied with official Press Releases, Press coverage invitations, notices, photographic material and other information by means of instant electronic dispatch. Arrangements are also made for local media representatives accompanying officials during official visits both inside America and abroad. The department also coordinates facilities afforded to the media during State functions, national events, and the General and Local events.

Photographic Services

Extensive photo coverage is given to Government activities as well as to national events. These services ensure fast transmission of current digital photographic material to the media.

Photography Archives

The archives house a vast collection of contemporary as well as historical photographic material which dates back to an era when it was founded. A selection of archived photos can be viewed at the Gallery.

Press Registry

The Department of Information has been housing the Press Registry where the register of newspapers, radio and TV stations is being kept and updated in terms of the Press Act. At the Press Registry, applications for registration purposes are submitted by editors and publishers of newspapers and periodicals, and by editors of radio and television stations; and certificates requesting confirmation of editorships to be deposited as evidence in libel cases brought before the Courts of Law, are prepared and issued over the signature of the Press Registrar.

Publishing
The department is responsible for the compilation and publication of the Government's News Paper, in its printed and electronic version. Other printed and electronic matter dealing with Government services and matters of public interest are also produced through this unit.

Sales Office
Publications sold by Official Government Publications, Budget Speeches, Financial Estimates and Economic Surveys and other viable publications. Photographs depicting a wide variety of topics such as International Meetings and Conferences held in the Palace, State and Official Visits, National Festivities, and National Heritage are also available for sale to the general public, as well as DVDs produced by the department.

Video Production
The department produces documentaries of national interest. The restoration, digitizing and archiving of historical film footage (16mm) is also a continuous process carried out by the department.

Once again, the amazing aspect about the basic operations of the **Ministry of Information** is that the NOI Original Instructions #3, given to the Laborers of Islam in 1934, detailed the importance of delivering correct information. It outlines the type of information to deliver concerning how to awaken new converts to Islam. It reads:

> "*Fulfillment of the Prophecies of All the Former Prophets concerning the Beginning of the Devils, and the Ending of the Civilization, and of our Enslavement by the Devils, and Present Time of our Delivery from the Devils by OUR SAVIOUR (ALLAH). PRAISE HIS HOLY NAME! There is No God but ALLAH. How that ALLAH would separate us from the Devils and, then destroy them; and Change us into a New and Perfect People; and Fill the Earth with FREEDOM, JUSTICE and EQUALITY as it was filled with wickedness; and Making we, the Poor Lost-Founds, the Perfect RULERS. The Laborers must Speak and Use grammatic pronunciation of words and syllables in Past, Future, Present and Perfect Tense. The Laborer's answers to All Lessons must be in the above Language. Others will not be considered.*"

Note: The Dumb must speak Plainly, the Stammering Tongue is Speaking Clear. (He covers the Prophecies of the Bible and, also, the Holy Qur'an in a word). NO man can be Successful in Teaching a People that cannot speak, Clearly, the People's Language.

But there is more to be understood in the words. That the Laborers' Pronunciation of words and syllables must be in the Past, Future and Present Perfect Tense - Otherwise will not be considered.

What is meant by the Laborers' answers to all LESSONS in the Past, Present and Future being PERFECT is that we must know and be Able to Prove, at all times, to the New Converts that the LESSONS that OUR SAVIOUR (ALLAH) gave us to Study and Learn is the Fulfillment of the Prophecies of All the Former Prophets concerning the Beginning of the Devils, and the Ending if the Civilization, and of our Enslavement by the Devils, and Present Time of our Delivery from the Devils by OUR SAVIOUR (ALLAH). PRAISE HIS HOLY NAME! There is No God but ALLAH. How that ALLAH would separate us from the Devils and, then destroy them; and Change us into a New and Perfect People; and Fill the Earth with FREEDOM, JUSTICE and EQUALITY as it was filled with wickedness; and Making we, the Poor Lost-Founds, the Perfect RULERS.

Therefore if we have not this Understanding, we are Yet Blind to HIM that has come to SAVE us. For this is OUR SAVIOUR'S Desire - that we should Know HIM as OUR GOD AND Saviour, and that Besides HIM there is NO SAVIOUR for us. [25]

Ministry of Art & Culture

What is a **Ministry of Arts and Culture**? It promotes supports, develops and protects the art culture, heritage, history of a nation, world history, ancient history and music to uplift the human spirit and energy. Also to improve socially, culturally and morally men, women and children's true self in relationship to Restrictive Law.

When you think about it, all of the above has been practically hidden from the general public when it concerns Art and Culture and what our progenitors have contributed to world affairs. This department also creates heritage sites, museums and monuments to assure history lives forever; free from misinterpretation by an enemies' perspective.

The Time is ripe for us to Re-claim our own, which is knowledge, understanding and a high civilization. We all are equipped physically and mentally to accomplish the said, above, with little study - young, old, men, women and children.

The M.G.T. & G.C.C. should study along with the Training. Report their progress along with the rest [26]

The Ministry of Science & Technology

What is a **Ministry of Science & Technology**? It is a governmental agency which performs the function of state management of science and technology, covering: scientific and technological activities; development of scientific and technological potential; intellectual property; standardization, measurement and quality control; atomic energy, radiation and nuclear safety; and state **management of public services** in the domains under its management in accordance with law.

After learning Mathematics, which is Islam, and Islam is Mathematics, it stands true. You can always prove it at no limit of time. Then you must learn to use it and secure some benefit while you are living, that is - luxury, money, good homes, friendship in all walks of life. [27]

Our universe is created in truth and reality, not falsified stories about monsters, good-tooth fairies and ol' Saint Nick. The God keeps it real, the Satan made-up stories about what is real.

Can't you see how every ministry needs qualified men and women to manage its overall function according an organizational chart? In some nations in the far east, each department may have Deputy Minister's to assure ministerial and administrative units serve the needs of the government and its citizens.

In 1935 on August 35th, the Honorable Elijah Muhammad wrote to his ministers of Islam:

"We should be well qualified, trained thoroughly, in what we are going to teach and is living that we teach, and fully submissive to our Saviour; whom we represent to the sleeping dead...Preach the truth of Islam; raise the dead, by telling them their Savior, has come, whom all the Prophets wrote and testified of..."

"Teaching who are Savior is, is the main object: That we must have (10,000) Fearing Moslems before we can be delivered, or see our King."[38]

Difference Between States, Nations And Nation-States

Again, we must ask the question: Is there a difference between a nation and a state? Emphatically Yes!

"A **nation** refers only to a socio-cultural entity, a union of people sharing who can identify culturally and linguistically. This concept does not necessarily consider formal political unions. "A **state** refers to a legal/political entity that is comprised of the following: a) a permanent population; b) a defined territory; c) a government; and d) the capacity to enter into relations with other states.

> "The growth in the number of nation-states means that nation-states are going to have to cope with new political, economic, and social realities. The new entrants in the political system bring with them new opportunities for the international political system, but also bring new problems that the international order must be able to approach and attempt to solve."[39]

Here is where each government has its own international representative and/or Secretary of the State (SOS). An important task for this office is to work to resolve

---

[38] Ministry Class Taught By The Most Honorable Elijah Muhammad Vol. 1
[39] http://www.towson.edu/polsci/ppp/sp97/realism/whatisns.htm

global issues. In brief, a SOS:

"Organizes and supervises the entire Department of State and the Government Foreign Service Laborers.

"Advises the Government Head on matters relating to foreign policy, including the appointment of diplomatic representatives to other nations, and on the acceptance or dismissal of representatives from other nations.

"Participates in high-level negotiations with other countries, either bilaterally or as part of an international conference or organization, or appoints representatives to do so. This includes the negotiation of international treaties and other agreements.

"Responsible for overall direction, coordination, and supervision of interdepartmental activities of the Government overseas.

"Providing information and services to citizens living or traveling abroad, including providing credentials in the form of passports and visas.

"Supervises the government immigration policy abroad.

"Communicates issues relating the Government foreign policy to Government Officials and to U.S. citizens."[40]

Of course, today's international order failed to solve its own world's political problems be it controlling their vassal states, vassal nation-states or subordinate governments. The main problem is their refusal to resolve what to do with 30 to 60 million Black people in North America.

No matter, at the appropriate time, when Black people become fully aware of who, what, when, where, how and why a nation of our own must be established and rooted in a Uniform Law of UNITY, a new Nation will press forward.

---

[40] http://www.state.gov/aboutstate/

The question is: Are the nations of the earth in transition toward a universal change? Are the human beings and people who implement the universal change in the world today or was he/they here 2000 years ago? [Isaiah 9:6] says, "*For a CHILD IS BORN to us, and a son is given to us, and the <u>government</u> is upon his <u>shoulder</u>: and his name shall be called, Wonderful, Counsellor, God the Mighty, the Father of the world to come, the Prince of Peace.*" The phrase shoulder is important. It means a certain people will have the highest authority in the government, and is a promise of unlimited power. It also denotes unlimited power will be conferred to God's ministers [Matthew 16:19]; and is applied also to Himself in Revelation 3:7. Without losing time, this information is all about the NOI and Black America's destiny. Not Rome—the Pope, nor Israel—the Zionist was meant to complete such prophecy although they are trying to make it so. After having 6,099 years to achieve their goal, by today's account it's been a catastrophic failure.

TEN

Qualify For Positions Awaiting You

*T*he Honorable Elijah Muhammad responded to the essential sciences and nationhood skills needed among Black people in North America in a letter he wrote to one of his followers on August 6, 1968.[41]

The Honorable Elijah Muhammad
Messenger of Allah
4847 South Woodlawn Avenue
Chicago, Illinois 60615
August 6, 1968

As-Salaam-Alaikum

In the Name of Almighty Allah, The Most Merciful Saviour, our Deliverer, who Came in the Person of Master Fard Muhammad, to whom praises are due forever, Master of the day of Judgment. To Allah alone do I submit and seek refuge.

Dear Brother:

I was so happy reading your letter dated July 10, 1968 of your contributions to the cause of Islam. I pray Allah will reward you so that you will not have any want for material things of this world. Regarding your education and striving towards an Engineers degree, **you have to get the knowledge from those that know.** If you want to work part of the time, and go to school part of the day, and you cannot arrange it differently, I say take it. If you are able to school yourself without trying to work at the same time on some job, I would look into that; because, **education is what the so-called Negro needs**. At the proper time we will need to know all types of Engineering. We

---

[41] http://www.muhammadspeaks.com/lettertomuhammadzahir.html

have to re-build for ourselves the type of Civilization that Allah demands us to accept. **In words to say--we have to rebuild a Nation. Engineering is the first trade that will be in demand.**

Thank you, may Allah bless you, and if there is anything the Nation can aid you in, feel not ashamed to ask any advice that you think is in us. Please do not hesitate in seeking the answer.

As-Salaam-Alaikum
Elijah Muhammad
Messenger of Allah
EM/vn/b2x

The Supreme Wisdom Book of Lessons given to Elijah Muhammad in 1931 by Master W. Fard Muhammad was designed to get future NOI members qualified to fulfill positions needed to transition into a New World of Peace and Righteousness on the foundation of Truth and Justice..One wherein wealth will be in abundance!

The Time is ripe for us to Re-claim our own, which is knowledge, understanding and a high civilization. *We all are equipped physically and mentally to accomplish the said, above, with little study - young, old, men, women and children*. [28]

A Ministry of Finance was mentioned in 1931 under the term Problem Book to get NOI members qualified to fulfill positions needed for a government and a future generation. That future is now! For example:

Supreme Wisdom Book Problem #11:

The Suez Canal in Egypt is ninety miles long, with a depth of thirty-three feet, and a width of one hundred twenty-two feet. The cost to build it sixty-four years ago was one hundred fifty million dollars. Mr. A. Ali has five hundred dollars worth of **stock** in it at the rate of six and three-fifths percent. Now he wants to know how much money he has coming to him at the above rate from 1869 to May 26, 1933...

Field of Study: catalactics

a) **Area of Study**: science of commercial exchange
b) **Derived Industries**: International Banks, Commercial Banks, Public Banks, Stock exchange, etc;
c) **Economic (or social benefit) potential**: (1) Holistic Intranationalism..(2) Friedrich Hayek used the term Catallaxy to describe a market economy. He was unhappy with the usage of the word "economy", feeling that the Greek root of the word - which translates as "household management" - implied that economic agents in a market economy possessed shared goals. Hayek derived the word Catallaxy from the Greek verb "katallassein" (or "katallattein") which meant not only "to exchange" but also "to admit in the community" and "to change from enemy into friend" (F.A. von Hayek, Law legislation and Liberty, Vol 2, 1976, pp. 108-109).

Lastly, the word **Stock** mentioned in Problem #11 opens up an entire world. The stock market directs one's mind to the science of **catalactics** (science of commercial exchange), if he or she is made aware of such a field of study. It also may direct one's mind to **notaphilly** (collecting of bank-notes) and how it affects the security and stability of any Money Matrix System.

To transmit these sciences into a reality, it begins with offspring who are well-trained, educated and qualified to establish national, intranational *(occurring or existing within a single nation and regions of that nation)* and global financial mechanisms to bring about balance to the universal economy.

Although stock exchanges do not exist to redistribute wealth; however, both casual and professional stock investors, through dividends and stock price increases that may result in capital gains. In our new government, wealth must be shared for the wealth of profitable national and local businesses.

All governments need a money matrix system, which means it needs a "priesthood" of righteous financial wizards. The basic entry qualification to produce such "priesthood" require applicants who must have specialized experience and/or directly related education in the amounts shown below:

d) **Education requirements**:

Accounting *4 years*
Auditing *2 years*
Advertising & Market Strategy *1 year*
Economics *4 years*
Laws & Taxation *4 years*
Foreign Language *2 years*
Foreign Trade Statics *4 years*
Mathematics *4 years*
Risk Management *4 years*
Production Market Research *4 years*
Interest & Exchange Rates *4 years*
Welfare & Reform *2 years*
Outsourcing *1 years*
Globalization *2 years*
Anti-trust Merging *4 years*
Commodity while dealing with stock and bond *4 years*
Mathematics *4 years*

Researching *2 years*
Investing *4 years*
Merging *4 years*
Signatures, Autographs, and Age *1 year*
Condition and Rarity *1 year*

A _Ministry of Health and Science_ was mentioned in the Supreme Book of Wisdom Book. For example:

Problem Book #1 – 6

1. The uncle of Mr. W.D. Fard lived in the wilderness of North America and he lived other than his own self, therefore, his pulse beat seventy-eight times per minute and this killed him in forty-five years of age. How many times did his pulse beat in forty-five years?

2. The wife of Mr. W.D. Fard's uncle, in the wilderness of North America, weighs other than herself, therefore, she has rheumatism, headaches, pain in all joints, and cannot walk up to the store. She is troubled frequently with high Blood pressure and registers more thirty-two. Her pulse is nearly eighty times per minute and she died at the age of forty-seven. How many times did her pulse beat in forty-seven years?

3. A Sheep contains fourteen square feet. One-tenth of a square inch contains fourteen thousand hairs. How many will the fourteen square feet contain?

4. One one-hundredth of a cubic inches contain two hundred million Atoms. How many will fifty square miles contain?

5. The uncle of Mr. W.D. Fard lives in the wilderness of North America and he is living other than himself, therefore, he weighs more than his height and his blood pressure registers more than thirty-two. This killed him at the age of forty-four years…

6. The second uncle of Mr. W.D. Fard, in the wilderness of North America, lived other than himself and, therefore, his blood pressure registered over thirty-two. He had fever, headaches, chills, grippe, hay fever, regular fever, rheumatism; also pain in all joints. He was disturbed with foot ailments and toothaches...If the air value selling price, then the third uncle of Mr. W.D. Fard would have been robbed of the Atmosphere. How much air did he breathe more than the average man? Each cubic foot of air costs $10.50.

How much does Mr. W.D. Fard's second uncle robbed in forty-six years? Twenty pills cost twenty-five cents. How much does this amount to in forty-six years?

Fields of Study *(ologies)* derived from *Problems 1 – 6*

Sphygmology: Study of the pulse
Symptomoatology: Study of symptoms of illness
Arthrology: Study of joints
Aceology: Therapeutics
Angiology: Study of blood flow and lymphatic system
Cardiology: Study of the heat
Desmology: Study of ligaments
Zoonomy: Animal physiology
Stoichiology: Science of elements of animal tissues
Trichology: Study of hair and its disorders
Somatology: Science of the properties of matter

The wealth of professions and industries derived from the aforementioned ologies are as follows under the title of Healthcare:

Dental Laboratories
General Medical and Surgical Hospitals
Health and Allied Services

Home Health Care Services
Intermediate Care Facilities
Kidney Dialysis Centers
Medical Laboratories
Nursing and Personal Care Facilities
Offices and Clinics of Chiropractors
Offices and Clinics of Dentists
Offices and Clinics of Doctors of Medicine
Offices and Clinics of Doctors of Osteopathy
Offices and Clinics of Health Practitioners
Offices and Clinics of Optometrists
Offices and Clinics of Podiatrists
Skilled Nursing Care Facilities,
Hospitals
Psychiatric Specialty Outpatient Facilities

All of the above signifies some form of medical school training and engineering.

A Ministry of Agriculture is mentioned in the Supreme Wisdom Book under the term Actual Facts. For example,

The Supreme Wisdom Book, Actual Fact #14 reads:

The producing land is 29,000,000 square miles.

Field of Study: *Agronomics*

a) ***Area of Study***: *Study of productivity of land*
b) ***Derived Industry***: *Soybeans* (**soybean industry**)
c) ***Economic (or social benefit) potential***: (1) *2005 72.1 million acres planted,* (2) *$16 Billion Farm cash receipts and production,* (3) *435 million bushels exported to China.* (4) *Employment* (5) *Grocery Store* (6) *Shipping and trucking* (7) *etc., etc.*

d) ***Educational requirements***: *Mathematics, Physical Life Science, Agricultural Science, Economics, Biology, Principles of Crop Production, etc;*

A Ministry of Defense is mentioned in the Supreme Wisdom Book of the Nation of Islam under Lost Found Muslim Lesson No.1. For example:

Lost Found Muslim Lesson No. 1, #12 – 14

12. What is the meaning of F.O.I.?
ANS.-The Fruit of Islam; the name given to the military training of the men that belong to Islam in North America.
13. What is the meaning of Lieu. and Capt.?
ANS.-Captain and Lieutenant. The duty of a captain is to give orders to the lieutenant, and the lieutenant's duty is to teach the private soldiers; also train them.
14. What is the meaning of M.G.T. and G.C.C?
ANS.-Muslim Girls' Training and General Civilization Class. This was the name given to the training of women and girls in North America; how to keep house, how to rear children, how to take care of their husbands, sew, cook, and, in general, how to act at home and abroad. ...

Fields of Study (ologies) derived from Lost Found Muslim Lesson No. 1, #12 – 14

Stratography: Art of leading an army
Polemology: Study of war
Aretaics: The science of virtue
Hygiatics: Study of development of character
Magirics: Art of cookery
Neonatology: Study of newborn babies
Oikology: Science of housekeeping
Paedology: Study of Children
Paedotrophy: Art of rearing children

Sexology: Study of sexual behavior
Proxemics: Study of man's need for personal space

<u>***A Ministry Of Science and Technology***</u> was mentioned in the Supreme Book of Wisdom Book beginning from problem 17. For example:

Problem Book #17 – 27

17. Mars, the inhabited Planet, is one hundred forty-one million, five hundred thousand miles from the Sun, and she travels one thousand thirty-seven and one-third miles per hour. Her diameter is four thousand two hundred miles.

18. Mercury is also an inhabited Planet and is thirty-six million miles from the Sun. Her diameter is three thousand miles…

24. Platoon is four billion, six hundred million miles from the Sun and she travels the same rate around the Sun as the rest of the Planets. It takes her three hundred forty-five years to make on complete circle around the Sun…

25. What is the Physical Standard of a devil against the original.
How many ounces of brain does an Original have?

27. The Universe Diameter equals seventy-six quintillion miles. What is the Area in Square miles. What is the Area in Square Yards? Give your answer in Figures only.

Fields of Study (ologies) derived from Problems # 17 – 27

Areology: Study of Mars
Planetology: Study of planets
Astrogeology: Study of extraterrestrial geology
Uranology: Study of the heavens; astronomy
Astronomy: Study of celestial bodies
Astrophysics: Study of behavior of interstellar matter

Astroseimology: Study of star oscillations
Uranography: Descriptive astronomy and mapping
Statics: Study of bodies and forces in equilibrium
Anthropobiology: Study of human biology
Cosmology: Study of the universe

You ask: what is the purpose of astronomy? Astronomy plays a much more practical role that is not nearly as important today as it was in the past. Since the time of our earliest ancestors, humans have used the motions of celestial objects to position themselves in space and time...

From the 19th century onwards, the Caucasian race has been using electromagnetic spectrums and the world of the atom on the development of astrophysics. This knowledge is a new discipline for them in astronomy that is now considered to be the most important to them.

Case in point, astronomy and physics classes may require a two-year cycle of 13, one-quarter courses.

Six courses are specifically required:
Astonomy 202, Electromagnetism and Plasma Physics
Astonomy 204A, Physics of Astrophysics I
Astonomy 204B, Physics of Astrophysics II
Astonomy 205, Introduction to Astronomical Research
Astonomy 220A, Stella Structure and Evolution
Astonomy 240A, Galactic and Extragalactic Stellar Systems

Not everyone will go on to work as an astrophysicists but such training will open the door to a whole range of other exciting and challenging careers. As a physicist a lot of opportunities will be open to you. Astrophysics courses are designed to enable one to develop skills in a number of areas useful for a career in science.

For example you will develop skills in problem solving and working together in a team. You will also learn many other things useful for a career in physics. Furthermore, you will learn about instrumentation, lasers, digital image processing, basic electronics and computer software development.

As a physicist, job prospects are good. Fields where you are likely to be employed as a physicist are:

Renewable energy (an increasingly important field)
Communications
Opto-electronics (lasers etc)
Materials science
Instrumentation (electronic measuring equipment)
Testing, Teaching
Medicine (eg. as a medical physicist)
Information Technology

Many government and industrial research laboratories and hospitals etc., employ physicists.[42]

But who wants to study and endure the *demanding* process of learning how to fulfill the task of God Knowledge- the mechanics of the universe?

One major problem with the educational system under white authority—Satan's system of government—is that it is profit driven. But not so in the New world of Islam, Inshallah (God willing), EDUCATION will be a part of the way of life and not in life's way saddled by student loan debt.

<u>**A Ministry of Justice**</u> was mentioned in the Supreme Book of Wisdom Book, Problem 30. For example:
30. The uncle of Mr. W.D. Fard lives in the wilderness of North America, surrounded and robbed completely by the Cave man. Therefore, he has no knowledge of his own nor anyone else's, but his mind travels twenty-four billion miles

---

[42] astrophysics.qut.edu.au/careers_for_physicists.asp

per second, which is considered the average speed of thought per second.

How many round trips will he make in ten seconds to the far Planet Platoon?

Fields of Study (ologies) derived from Problem #30

Victimology: Study of victims*[43]
Nomology: The science of the laws; especially of the mind
Metaphysics: Study of principles of nature and thought
Metapsychology: Study of nature of mind
Psychobiology: Study of biology of the mind
Psychology: Study of mind
Psychophysics: Study of link between mental and physical processes

Lesson 30 of the Problem Book is clearly a subject about Justice for victims of crime like it states, *"The uncle of Mr. W.D. Fard lives in the wilderness of North America, surrounded and robbed completely by the Cave man."* How does crime, victims of crime and perpetrators of crime think and feel? Does one or both reflect a symptom of a damaged mind?

That's why neuroscience or study of the mind is important for a nation to understand how the human mind thinks and what may ill-effect it away from thinking into the mind of God.

25. What is the meaning of crime be it government or otherwise and how has it ill-affected or influenced your mind and the fall of western civilization?

---

[43] *Victimology is the study of victimization, including the relationships between victims and offenders, the interactions between victims and the criminal justice system

Without going further, I think the message is clear how the original Supreme Wisdom Book of the Nation of Islam was pre-written for preparation. Allah, God, Himself, is preparing present and future generations to transition establish a New world of Islam (Kingdom of peace) by the time and what is going to be done through its structure. Therefore, the question registered members of the Lost and Found Nation of Islam and Black America should consider is this: Are we resolute with qualifications right down to the modern times? After all, time is serving us for it is a creation of Allah, The Originator *(AL-MUBDI')*.[44] The God of Islam has no beginning nor ending. *"If we learn ourselves, learn the universe, we learn Allah, <u>we learn ourselves.</u>"*

"The American white race doesn't want the so-called Negroes to believe in the religion of Islam, but the poor lost-found Members of the tribe of Shabazz are now learning very fast. Islam is TRUTH but what they (Caucasians) hate the most is the teaching of the true knowledge of themselves…

"…This country is now being plagued by Allah: Storms, Hail, Snow, and Earthquakes.

"My people ISLAM IS YOUR SALVATION. The devil desires to frighten you away from accepting Islam. Don't let him do that, for Allah is well able to protect you and me from the evil planning.

"**Hurry and join onto your Own kind. The Time of this World is at Hand.**"[29]

---

[44] Arabic meaning: The originator, He who has created for the first time all beings from nothing and without any model.

ELEVEN

Farrakhan More Than A Statesmen

Definition of *STATESMAN* 1: one versed in the principles or art of government; ***especially***: one actively engaged in conducting the business of a government or in shaping its policies, 2: a wise, skillful, and respected political leader.

Who is FARRAKHAN? Well, you can tell who a man is by his works, can't you…

Amidst the Great Depression, Min. Louis Farrakhan was born Louis Eugene Walcott on May 11, 1933, in New York City. At the age of 3, he and his family moved to Boston, Mass. He is the son of Sumayyah Farrakhan (born Sara Mae Manning—see picture on page 132) and Percival Clarke, whom he did not meet. His mother reared him and his brother Alvan in a highly disciplined and spiritual household. At an early age, his mother exposed him to music, art, culture and history. Black newspapers and magazines like the *Crisis* were popular in his household. His mother, at great personal sacrifice, sponsored her children's music education, Alvan on piano and Louis on violin.

In his young teens, Min. Farrakhan performed with the Boston College Orchestra and the Boston Civic Symphony. After graduating from the prestigious Boston Latin High School, he entered Winston-Salem Teachers College in North Carolina, on an academic and athletic scholarship, majoring in English. At 19, sophomore at Winston-Salem Teachers College was selected to play his violin on the

Horace Heidt show, "The America Way"...on February 26, 1953.

Sumayyah Farrakhan
Mother of Minister Louis Farrakhan Muhammad

In September 1953, during his senior year, he married his childhood sweetheart, Betsy Jean, who is today known as Mother Khadijah Farrakhan. To support his young family, he left college and began his career in show business. On the performing arts stage he became known as "The Charmer" and was highly acclaimed as a vocalist, actor, musician and composer. Commentators, during the 1950s, acknowledged his versatility and deftness in all the popular genres of the time including calypso, classical, jazz and blues. While on tour appearing at the prestigious Chicago supper club, Gene Sperling's Blue Angel, a friend from Boston invited young Louis to attend the Nation of Islam's 1955 Saviour's Day convention. Upon hearing the message of the Honorable Elijah Muhammad, he immediately accepted it along with his wife. After writing his letter to become a registered member of the Nation of Islam, Louis Eugene Walcott became Louis X.

"From year 1955, Louis X arose in the ranks of Islam in New York City under Minister Malcolm X. He gave up his career in show business and dedicated his life to advance the religion of Islam. As a fundraiser for the Nation of Islam combined with spreading the message of his leader, Louis X debuted as a playwright, producer and actor in his original play, "Orgena," on the stage of New York's prestigious Town Hall Theater in 1960. Around the same time, he recorded the hit song, "A White Man's Heaven Is A Black Man's Hell."

After receiving his "basic training," Min. Malcolm X under the guidance of the Honorable Elijah Muhammad dispatched the then-Louis X to Boston to serve as captain, the coordinator of men's affairs. Soon thereafter, he was elevated to the post of minister and served from 1956 to

1965 at Muhammad's Temple No. 11.

"In the aftermath of the assassination of Malcolm X, the Honorable Elijah Muhammad reassigned Louis X to New York City over Mosque #7 as its Minister, gave him the name Farrakhan and later promoted him as his National Representative. The New York scene quickly was transformed by the ever-widening Muslim presence. Every borough and suburb of the city was bustling with members of the Nation of Islam. Temples, schools, businesses and community rehabilitation programs could be found all over the city. Also during the 60s and 70s, on behalf of the Honorable Elijah Muhammad, Min. Farrakhan began his radio ministry in New York and all over the country."

By 1972, the Honorable Elijah Muhammad opened a $2 million mosque and school in Chicago. During this important grand opening of Temple No. 2, as it was known then, he praised and let it be known who his top helper was in his work. He asked Minister Farrakhan to come before the religious community and then made the following announcement while digressing from his previously stated remarks: "I want you to remember, today, I have one of my greatest preachers here. ... What are you hiding behind the sycamore tree for brother? (He chuckled.) C'mon around here where they can see you!" (A rousing round of applause ensued). "We have with us today," Mr. Muhammad continued, <u>"our great national preacher. The preacher who don't mind going into Harlem, New York, one of the most worst towns in our nation or cities. It is our brother in Detroit and Chicago or New York. But, I want you to remember every week he's on the air helping me to reach those people that I can't get out of my house and go reach them like he. I want you to pay good attention to his preaching. His preaching is a bearing of witness to me and what God has given to me,"</u> he declared. <u>"This is one of the strongest national preachers that I have in the bounds of North America. Everywhere you hear him, listen to him. Everywhere you see him, look at him. Everywhere he advises you to go, go. Everywhere he advises you to stay from, stay from. For we are thankful to Allah for this great</u>

helper of mine, Minister Farrakhan." (Another rousing round of applause ensued). "He's not a proud man," he said. "He's a very humble man. If he can carry you across the lake without dropping you in; he don't say when you get on the other side, 'You see what I have done?' He tells you, 'You see what Allah has done.' He doesn't take it upon himself. He's a mighty fine preacher. We hear him every week, and I say continue to hear our Minister Farrakhan. ..." [30]

By 1974, Black America's love of the Nation of Islam grew into one of that decade's largest mass meetings of its kind on Randall's Island where Min. Farrakhan delivered the "Black Family Day" address before 70,000.

Who is FARRAKHAN in comparison with those greats mentioned in Mecca, Arabia's divine Islamic history?

"1,400 years ago Prophet Mohammed stated to his followers, according to a hadith on the day (of the assembly) at his house, especially to the Banu (tribe of) Abd Al-Muttalib: He said: "Whoever helps me in this matter will be my brother, my testamentary trustee (wasi) my helper (wazir), my heir and my successor after me." His cousin Ali said, "O Apostle of God, I will help you." Then the Prophet said, "Sit down, you are my brother, my trustee, my helper, my inheritor and successor after me." In addition the Prophet said at Ghadir Khumm (a pond situated on the Incense Route between Syria and Yemen: "Am I not more appropriate for authority over you than yourselves?" Then he spoke to them (his followers) in an ordered manner without any interruption in his speech and required for (Ali), through laying down obedience to him and his authority (over the believers), the same authority as he had over them, and which he made them acknowledge and which they did not deny."

QUESTION: How do the comments made by Prophet Mohammed regarding the nomination of Ali for the succession to his position to lead the promising Islamic nation 1,400 years ago relate to what the Honorable Elijah Muhammad said about Minister Farrakhan in 1972 during the grand opening of Muhammad's Temple No.2? Furthermore, whatever confusion that has remained in the holy land of Mecca, Arabia about our last prophet Mohammed and Ali; none remains in North America about Elijah and Farrakhan because these two fulfilled that history by Allah's Divine Active Will. Only the envious and half-learned bark at the moon concerning their event during these end times.[31]

Return of Farrakhan

In 1975, after it was announced that the Honorable Elijah Muhammad died at Chicago Mercy Hospital, his son Imam Warith Deen Mohammed (PBBH) took the reign to govern the Nation of Islam and changed its name to the World Community of al-Islam in the West. Then two years later, in 1977, he changed the name of his organization to the American Muslim Mission/World Community of al-Islam. This change of direction required that Minister Farrakhan ultimately re-establish the NOI; in which he achieved, September, 1977. His time to leave and to return to the original structure of the NOI was prewritten in the Supreme Wisdom Book of the NOI, problem 31, prepared by Allah (God), in the Personage of Master W. Fard Muhammad. It reads:

"He also has seventeen million keys, which he turns at the rate of sixteen and seventeen one-hundredths per minute. How long will it take him to turn the whole seventeen million? Sixty minutes equal one hour. Twenty-four hours equal one day. Three hundred sixty-five days equal one year."

After completing the word math problem 31, you will find it takes 2 years to turn seventeen million keys at said rate mentioned above. The 2 years are applied to the time it took Minister Farrakhan to return to his rightful place as leader of the Nation of Islam after Elijah Muhammad escaped the death plot in Mercy Hospital, February, 1975. (2 years + 1975 = 1977)

From 1975 to September 1977 is also 30 months. Read the Holy Quran 3:85 and 27:30, along with Bible John 2:19-20. What you shall read is how the Original Ancient Black Scientists of Islam understood the value of Minister Farrakhan's life and mission. How they calculated seeing his divine work open out 46 years after the first meeting took place between Elijah Muhammad and the Great Mahdi, Master W. Fard Muhammad. [1931 + 46 years = 1977]

Next, as it was prewritten, in 1978, nearly three years after Elijah Muhammad's departure, **FARRAKHAN** began traveling the country to [re]build a network of relationships and study groups that would begin the Nation of Islam's *second resurrection*, like the Quran says for "*a people who disbelieved after their believing, and after they had borne witness that the Messenger was true, and clear arguments had come to them?*"

Then in 1981, FARRAKHAN then hosted the first Saviour's Day convention from the time after the NOI was overthrown in 1975. Subsequently, he traveled 300,000 miles to nearly 50 U.S. cities in 1981 spreading the life giving teachings of Islam of the Honorable Elijah Muhammad. New frontiers and alliances were forged in the years to come.

After Rev. Jesse L. Jackson, Sr. announced his plan to run for president of the United States in 1983, Min. Farrakhan became a member of the steering committee. By 1985, African heads of state offered their support and assistance to the Nation of Islam. Libya's leader, Col. Muammar Gadhafi, in 1985 loaned the Nation of Islam a $5 million interest free loan. Rapid progress continued in the rebuilding of the Nation of Islam and by 1992, 60,000 people attended Saviours' Day in Atlanta at the newly opened Georgia Dome. Likewise, in 1994, the first Saviours' Day convention outside of the United States was convened in Accra, Ghana, West Africa. In Washington, D.C., on Monday, Oct. 16, 1995, nearly two million black men who came to hear Minister Louis Farrakhan speak attended the Million Man March.

The March was dedicated to Allah and included the themes of atonement, personal responsibility and reconciliation.

In 1997 the Minister opened a 52-nation world "friendship" tour in Baghdad, defying U.S. warnings that his visits to countries considered terrorist states could be used for propaganda purposes.

In November 1999, he and his National Board met a delegation of Jewish leaders at their request—initially to seek help in the release of Jewish rabbis in Iran suspected of spying for Israel—to begin to build a bridge for dialogue between the Nation of Islam and the Jewish community. He convened a press conference of religious leaders in December 1999 to continue his call for religious harmony and proper celebration of religious holy days. The Final Call Newspaper in following words even covered this:

At THE NATIONAL HOUSE Of the Nation of Islam—The meeting began with prayers—one in Hebrew, another in Arabic—and then a spirited and spiritual dialogue began between the leader of the Nation of Islam and seven members of the **Neturei Karta International orthodox Jewish community.** The historic meeting occurred Nov. 9 at the home of the Honorable Elijah Muhammad in Hyde Park, a quiet and diverse Chicago community inhabited by Muslims, Christians and Jews, blacks and whites. *"On behalf of the Nation of Islam, I am honored to have you in the home of the Honorable Elijah Muhammad,"* the Honorable Minister Louis Farrakhan said, extending a warm welcome to the **Jewish delegation led by Rabbi Moshe Beck**.

> *"We have believed all along that a day like this would come. The Honorable Elijah Muhammad hinted to us in one of his writings that the problem between the Jewish community and us in the United States would be worked out. So we believe that this (meeting) is not accidental ... this is a part of God's divine planning for us," Min. Farrakhan said.*

The meeting was a follow-up to an earlier meeting that was quietly held June 9, when the delegation visited Chicago for a meeting with the Nation of Islam Board chaired by Chief of Staff Leonard F. Muhammad. That meeting concerned the arrest at that time of members of the Jewish community in Iran who were accused of spying for Israel. At that time, the Jewish delegation appealed for whatever helps the Nation of Islam could provide in seeking a resolution to the crisis.

"The Nov. 9 meeting, however, was not to focus on the Iranian Jews, said Rabbi David Weiss, spokesman for the group who translated for senior Rabbi Moshe Beck, but to "sanctify God's name ...to clarify what is a Jew ...and what our position is to all the nations of the world and, specifically, what our position is to the Nation of Islam and to the revered Honorable Minister Farrakhan."

"Rabbi Beck's opening prayer called for God's blessing upon Min. Farrakhan for "long life and healthy years to continue preaching the truth and doing good deeds."

"After the prayers, the delegation presented the Minister with a plaque stating:

> "May God bless you and safeguard you. May God illuminate His countenance for you and be gracious to you. May God turn His countenance to you and establish peace for you. Presented with the deepest respect to the Honorable Minister Louis Farrakhan by the representatives of Torah Jewry."
>
> "Rabbi Weiss explained that the words are a traditional blessing for a king or nobility.

"Explaining that orthodox Jews strictly follow the Torah, **Rabbi Weiss said his community and other orthodox Jews lead simple lives absent of many of the material items of the world such as televisions. He said they are bound by their holy book to be humble and peaceful and to be loyal citizens, obedient to the rulers of the land in which they live. He said they regretted that some members of the Jewish community had attacked Min. Farrakhan and vilified his name in the media, and that the orthodox community should have spoken out against the attack.**

> *"Rabbi Fryman said the meeting with Min. Farrakhan "is a landmark that should have come about earlier."*
>
> *"A major problem for orthodox Jews, said Rabbi Beck, is the Zionists during the early days of the establishment of the State of Israel used scare tactics and propaganda to convince the orthodox community that if Israel was not successful, then Arabs and anti-Semites would further persecute Jews.*
>
> *"Rabbi Beck, through translation, said that attacks on some synagogues in the Middle East were carried out by Israeli terrorists and blamed on Arabs…*

"After these comments, the Honorable Minister Farrakhan went on the say:

> **"Minister. Farrakhan said Muslims are bound to respect the people of the Book because to do so is to respect Him who revealed the Book. He said Muslims also respect Jewish houses of worship and "any house where the one God is worshipped."**
>
> *"This is why no matter what we have suffered from the misrepresentation of the Zionist-controlled media, you have never heard of an incident where one of my followers ever attacked a person …because of their faith tradition," he said.*
>
> *"Min. Farrakhan defined a Jew as someone with a unique and special covenant with God who is bound by obedience to the laws of the Torah. But he also warned that whenever God reveals His word to a people, "that wisdom and revelation becomes a trial for those who receive it. If we use the wisdom to oppose God's law, God's commandments, then the wisdom of the revelation causes us to become Satanic," he said.*

"Encouraging the rabbis to be more vocal in their opposition to falsehood, Min. Farrakhan said America is being destroyed because of its moral degeneracy and the destruction of the family. He said only the family values taught in the Torah, Injil (Gospel) and the Holy

Qur'an, "properly administered and fought for" will save America from a destruction that "will make Sodom and Gomorra ...look like child's play. "Satan is winning because the righteous are divided and are weak. Sometimes the righteous are cowardly in that we are afraid to stand up for God so He can prove that even though we are small in number, He will make us prevail over armies as He showed you the history of the Children of Israel," he said.

> *"We do not believe that Jesus of 2000 years ago was the Messiah. We believe the Messiah was yet to come, and this is the time period that the Messiah would make himself manifest," Min. Farrakhan said.*

"He added that his teacher, the Hon. Elijah Muhammad, told his followers to study the history of the Jewish people because it is full of lessons for Blacks in America who have suffered a 400-year bondage "unlike the slavery of other human beings. After 400 years, (God) gave them Moses, the liberator," he said. "And we, too, believe that Allah has been merciful to us and it is our time now to come out of exile, but it is also your time as well. We believe that Elijah, who was to come before that great and dreadful day of the Lord ...has come into the world, not only to turn our hearts back to our fathers, but to turn the hearts of the people of the Book, who have strayed from the path of God, turn them back, because only in turning us back to the path of God can we truly come out of exile and again be called the people of God," he said.

"Beginning in early December 1997, Louis Farrakhan and his 24-member delegation embarked upon the third "World Friendship Tour."

"Farrakhan stated that he "..would like to demonstrate how diplomacy and friendly relations should be carried out" while paying visits to 52 nations on the tour; in the end, the total number of nations visited was 37. Africa, the Middle East, Asia, Russia, the Far East, Australia, and Cuba were among the areas visited by Farrakhan and his delegation. **He met with 13 heads of state, a few heads of**

government, prime ministers, foreign ministers, ministers of information, ministers of trade and commerce, deputy foreign ministers, scholars of every type. Below are actual pictures of whom he met.

Photos of 1997 World Tour

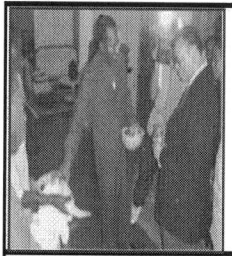	**Mali** Mali President Alpha Oumar Konare presents Min. Farrakhan with traditional gifts.
	**Palestine/Israel** President Arafat presents Min. Farrakhan with sculpture, "Mother-of-Pearl".
	**Egypt** The Hon. Minister Louis Farrakhan is pictured with Shaykh Mohammed Sayed Tantawi, Grand Shaykh of Al-Azar University, in Egypt.
	**Libya** Muammar Qadhafi, the former leader of the Libyan in picture with Minister Louis Farrakhan.

Russia and Daghestan
In Mahachkala, the capital of the Caucasus Mountain region of Daghestan, Min. Farrakhan and his delegation encountered a spirit and zeal that exceeds that of the Muslims anywhere he has traveled outside of the United States, the Nation of Islam leader said, pointing out that a woman from that same mountain region was the Mother of Master W.D. Fard.

Liberia
Min. Farrakhan meets with President Charles Ghankay Taylor of Liberia.

South Africa
Min. Farrakhan receives a new flag of The Democratic Republic of The Congo from Prime Minister Abdoulaye Yerodia. He is the first Muslim in the Congolese government since independence, and it was his first day on the job, his first official visitor was Min. Farrakhan.

Sudan
The Honorable Minister Louis Farrakhan, right is greeted by Dr. Hassan Turabi, the speaker of Sudan's Parliament Jan. 16 during the Minister's stop in Sudan, part of his World Friendship Tour.

Malawi
Joyous throngs of well-wishers greet Min. Farrakhan at Kotoka Intl. Airport during the World Friendship Tour III's recent stop in Accra, Ghana.

Phillipines
The Honorable Minister Louis Farrakhan (left) greets Bangladeshi Muslims after Friday Jumah (congregation) prayer Feb. 6 in Dhaka, Bangladesh. Min. Farrakhan was invited to Bangladesh by the International Islamic Representation Organization and met with religious and political leaders.

Australia
More than 100 cheering supporters--Muslims, Aborigines, Blacks--waited over four hours at Sydney Airport to provide a 30-vehicle-escort to take the Nation of Islam leader and his entourage to the Imam Ali Mosque in the mostly-Muslim Lakemba Residential District, where another 1,000 supporters waved banners and shouted "Allah-hu Akbar (God is Great)," when Minister Farrakhan arrived.

Cuba
Hon. Minister Louis Farrakhan, President Fidel Castro.

Gambia
Min. Farrakhan and President Yahya Jammeh, of Gambia, discuss issues during the Minister's World Friendship Tour III.

These photos represent only 1 of 3 world tours completed by the Honorable Minister Farrakhan Muhammad. Those whom he encountered evinced that he does carry the NOI government on his shoulders.

His most recent tour of 2012 was in the Caribbean to

[re]arouse them to unite as One Great Island Nation. A brief history of this possibility is as follows:

• **The Federation of the West Indies (1958-1962):** The 10-member group included Antigua, Barbados, Grenada, Dominica, Jamaica, Montserrat, St. Kitts/Nevis, St. Vincent, St. Lucia, and Trinidad & Tobago. The aims were to strengthen the movement for self-government, to promote economic development and to safeguard democracy. The W.I. Federation facilitated the movement from colonialism to independence. But this united effort collapsed within a few short years.

• **CARIFTA Caribbean Free Trade Area (1968-1973):** It had 11 members—Antigua, Barbados, Guyana, Dominica, Jamaica, Montserrat, St.Kitts/Nevis, St. Vincent, St. Lucia, Trinidad & Tobago and Belize. Only Grenada from the Federation was not involved, and Guyana and Belize, both non-islands were added. The aims of CARIFTA were to foster economic and social development by encouraging free trade which involved the removal of previous customs duties, taxes and licensing arrangements.

• **CARICOM (1973):** CARIFTA was transformed into CARICOM in 1973 and included all 11 members of CARIFTA as well as the Bahamas, Haiti, Suriname and Grenada. The major objectives of CARICOM are political integration through the coordination and merging of foreign policy among member states; economic integration and cooperation and functional cooperation, for example in health, education, law, disaster relief, agriculture, culture, communications, financial and industrial relations and other services.

• **OCES The Organization of Eastern Caribbean States (1981):** Group was established June 18, 1981 with the signing of a treaty between seven countries—Antigua, Dominica, Grenada, Montserrat, St. Kitts, St. Lucia and St. Vincent. The OECS sought to promote development by the formation of a common market among member states and to deal more efficiently with international bodies.

• **ACS The Association of Caribbean States (1995):** For the first time leaders brought together the English, Spanish, French and Dutch speaking Caribbean nations, and sought to promote increased economic activity by trading raw materials and finished products among members. There are 25 member states, three associate members and 14 observer countries (including Egypt, India, Italy, Korea, Russia and Spain). The collective population of the ACS is 210 million people. Treaties are often signed between member nations for the development of trade, exchange of technology, as well as cultural and educational pursuits.

• **CSME Caribbean Single Market & Economy (2006 to present):** The CARICOM Single Market and Economy is an integrated development strategy to unite economies and markets of participating countries. The idea was envisioned in July 1989 in Grenada. The desire was to allow for unrestricted movement of citizens as visitors, traders, skilled persons, entrepreneurs or job seekers. The CSME is being implemented through a number of phases, beginning with the CARICOM Single Market (CSM). The CSM was initially implemented on January 1, 2006 with the signing of the document for its implementation by six original member states. [32]

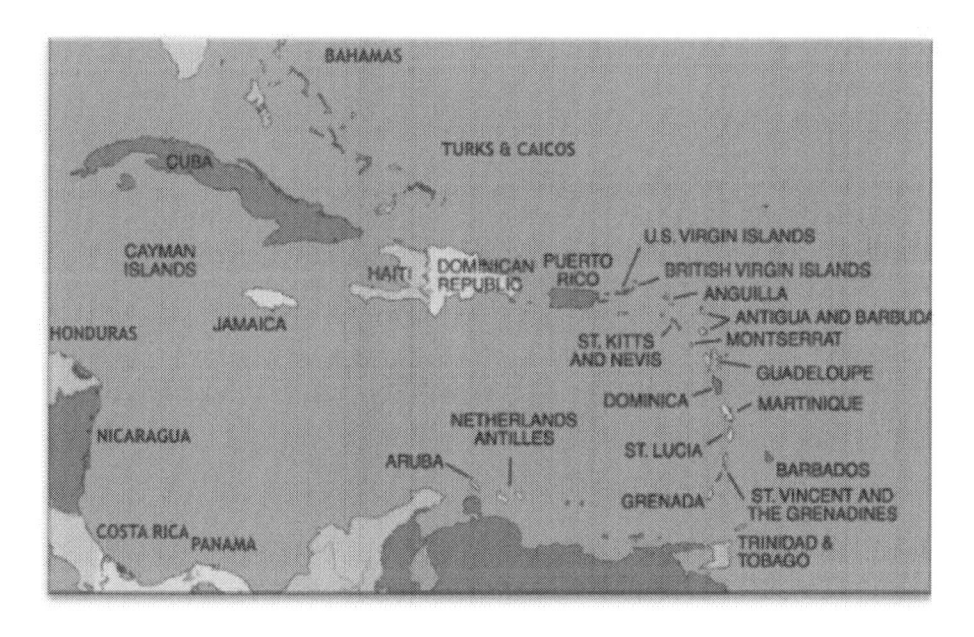

To reignite this great endeavor, **Minister Farrakhan's** recent tour throughout the Caribbean is urging political leaders to take steps towards forming a New Caribbean

Federation according to a great prophecy.

"The stop in Barbados followed arriving in Grenada, where the trip started Nov. 22. The Minister met with the Honorable Tilman Thomas, prime minister of Grenada, and Opposition Leader Keith Mitchell.

"In St. George's, the Minister called for greater unity in the Caribbean before a lecture Nov. 24 at the Grenada Trade Centre.

"Grenada cannot exist independent of other Caribbean islands. So, the future of the West Indies must just not just stop with CARICOM, but there must be a political union of the whole of the Caribbean," said Farrakhan, according to published reports.

The Minister also met Nov. 23 for an hour with the Honorable Tilman Thomas, at the official residence of Grenada's prime minister. As they shook hands, the prime minister shared how he once lived in New York and listened to Min. Farrakhan speak Sundays on radio station WLIB.

Photo: Richard Simon/Prime Minister's Office Grenada

"The N.O.I. leader also paid special tribute to assassinated former Grenada Prime Minister Maurice Bishop and to Malcolm X, reported Spiceislander.com. "Grenada gave us Malcolm; Grenada gave us Mr. Bishop," Farrakhan said, according to the Nov. 23 article.

"All of us in America who are nationalistic in our thinking, we loved Bishop. We saw him as a very progressive mind."

"Min. Farrakhan also said its time for all countries—"including the U.S. and Grenada— to end the practice of partisan party politics, which is hampering national development," said Spiceislander.com.

"We need to think more of Grenada and the Caribbean rather than our party," he said. "Our party is important; but our party is not more important than the nation that these parties are to serve."

"Min. Farrakhan's schedule includes stops in Dominica, the U.S. Virgin Islands, Belize, and the Bahamas."[45]

Minister Farrakhan greets the Hon. Freundel Stuart, prime minister of Barbados, during a courtesy call at government headquarters in St. Michael. Photo: Barbados Government Information Service

White People In The New World of The Righteous

The following words are taken from the Table Talks with our Beloved Messenger pages 5-6. It begins as such:

"**Question:** What do we mean when we say white or black? What constitutes a white person and what constitutes Black? What do we mean when we use the term Negro? In certain areas of the world, if you have a certain amount of black blood in you it makes you a Negro according to their classifications. In other areas of the world, a little white blood makes you white. How do we clearly define such relationships? How do we say whom we accept or don't accept? Do we let these people in the Mosque? What do we teach them related to Islam?

---

[45] http://www.finalcall.com/artman/publish/World_News_3/article_9381.shtml

Answer: We can accept belief from anyone regardless to what color they may be if they believe. We can accept belief in them or on the merit of their belief but it does not mean we should house them under the same roof of our place of worship as an equal member with us. The reason for this is because we have been rejected by the societies of all colors of people and we have suffered wearing the shackles of slavery and abject ones amongst the Nations. Therefore Allah has chosen us to be his selected people and therefore making us a selected or elected people of His, He does not want us to mix with those who have rejected us until He has made us what He wants us to be. What He wants us to be is head and rule over them that have destroyed us as a ruling power and as an equal member of their society.

Therefore Allah intends to make us now a better people and have a greater society and in the reverse reject them (those that have rejected us) for He will guide us, teach us of Himself, His wisdom and His wisdom is superior to any of the known rulers knowledge. So it is true that the Bible teaches that we are his elect because he wants to make a new people of nothing. We are the only people on earth that are rejected by all other civilized societies of the Nations of the earth. That means we are outcasts. Allah want to show the world how great and wise He is. Allah takes the outcast and teaches and trains the outcast to become the rulers of the rulers to fulfill the Bible wherein it says you are no longer the tail but now the head and in the stone that the builders reject: it only means a people that some civilization rejected and now He has made that people the Head. Now, to build a new Nation Allah uses these rejected people for his cornerstone.

Question: Does this refer specifically to the Negro here in America? The West Indian for example, does this include them? They have come from the Islands and..........

Answer: West Indians are still our people only they were ruled under other than the American white man. They were ruled under the British but they are too drifters out of Africa.

"We will soon make a try at converting and uniting all the originals of this Western Hemisphere." *(Messenger of Allah,*

Message to the Blackman-chapter 91-----1963)

So it appears that any universal government must flourish and succeed with all offices of such government operating under divine wisdom, knowledge and understanding by the best people in government and civic comprehension for all.

Is it not true that all government policy and procedural issues are local, regional, national and international? Therefore; should the question be: Can the best people unite to resolve issues by getting to know each other diplomatically.

26. What is the role of a diplomat?

_____
_____
_____
_____
_____
_____
_____
_____

Latino's In The Nation of Islam

A Universal Government is the only divine solution for all people that we may know each other in righteousness for our good deeds and actions. The Muslim book of scripture says, [Quran 49:13-14] "*O mankind, surely We have created you from a male and a female, and made you tribes and families that you may know each other. The bedouins say, "'We have believed.'" Say, "'You have not [yet] believed; but* say [instead], "'We have submitted,'" for faith has not yet entered your hearts. And if you obey Allah and His Messenger, He will not deprive you from your deeds of anything. Indeed, Allah is Forgiving and Merciful."

When Master W. Fard Muhammad completed the Supreme Wisdom Book's Student Enrollment, He posed two questions:

1. Who is the Original man?
2. Who is the Colored man?

The answer is:

1. The original man is the Asiatic Black man; the Maker; the Owner; the Cream of the planet Earth - Father of Civilization, God of the Universe.

2. The Colored man is the Caucasian (white man). Or, Yacub's grafted Devil - the Skunk of the planet Earth.

3. The population of the Original nation in the wilderness of North America is 17,000,000.

- ☐ With the 2,000,000 Indians makes it - 19,000,000.
- ☐ All over the planet Earth is 4,400,000,000.

4. The population of the Colored people in the wilderness of North America is 103,000,000

- ☐ All over the planet Earth is 400,000,000.[46]

---

[46] http://www.thenationofislam.org/Studentenrollment.html

"How do members of the Black community view this critical aspect of the Honorable Elijah Muhammad's teaching, particularly since commentators and academics have categorized the Nation of Islam as a "Black nationalist" organization? How does this relate to the rise of Islam among Latinos? Minister Farrakhan continues, "In Message To The Black Man and in the Muhammad Speaks and elsewhere, the Honorable Elijah Muhammad wrote much on the Native American and their rise to divine prominence, along with the Black man. He did much too. For example, he placed a part of his family in Mexico. He established at least five Temples or places where his teachings were delivered in Mexico."

"There are several significant events in the history of the Nation of Islam where this relationship between Blacks and the Native American and Hispanic peoples was solidified. One early account of this is the friendship of the Honorable Elijah Muhammad with Henry Almanza Sr., a Mexican living in Detroit who had married a Black American woman, Mary Almanza. Mary Almanza, along with her 10 children, had become some of the early members of Detroit's Temple #1 under Master Fard Muhammad. She became one of the first teachers in the University of Islam, even being arrested during the raids on the Temple. Her husband, who immigrated to the U.S. after the Mexican revolution, dined with the Honorable Elijah Muhammad frequently and was a great supporter of his cause, although never registering in the Temple himself.

"Later on in his work, the Honorable Elijah Muhammad further demonstrated his desire for unity through his relocation to Phoenix, where he was known to frequently visit and meet with the Indigenous Nations of the region. He established diplomatic ties with the government of Peru for the importing of Whiting H&G and worked extensively with land sovereignty activist, Reies Lopez Tijerina, whom he commissioned as an emissary to the Mexican government on his behalf. His final relocation, before his departure was to a home in Mexico.

"As Allah's Nation in the wilderness of North America grew, the repression and abuse from America's race struggles naturally drew

Blacks and Hispanics together, with many finding refuge within the ranks of the Nation of Islam. By the 1950s many Caribbean born Latinos and Central Americans had served in the movements New York Mosque while on the West Coast a number of Mexicans became among the first Hispanics to embrace Islam. Mexican pioneers of the Nation of Islam included Brother Benjamin X Perez (Imam Benjamin Perez Mahoma) of Oakland, a friend of farm worker Activist Cesar Chavez; Minister Emanuel X Villalobos of Los Angeles who spoke during Saviour's Day 1968; and Manuel X Alva who established an outpost in Tijuana, Mexico.

Cesar Chavez holding a copy of Muhammad Speaks. This photo ran with an interview in the August 4, 1972 edition.

"The seeds of this unity planted by the Great Mahdi were now budding and coming into fruition under the leadership of the Honorable Elijah Muhammad and his young National Representative of Caribbean parentage, Minister Louis Farrakhan. It was through the articulation of these teachings by the Honorable Minister Louis Farrakhan that many Latinos embraced Islam, as well as impacting the Hispanic community outside of the Nation."[47]

The transition of the original people and oppressed people to attain a complete freedom cannot be stopped no matter where we reside on earth! A universal change is here!

Evincing enough, the Lost and Found members of the

---

[47] http://www.finalcall.com/artman/publish/Perspectives_1/article_9164.shtml

Nation of Islam in the West are demonstrating "best practices" in utilizing Allah's wisdom, knowledge and understanding to be an example for all communities; and, no that greater is yet approaching by the divine guidance coming through the Honorable Minister Louis Farrakhan Muhammad. [Quran 13:11] *"Shifts (of angels) take turns, staying with each one of you—they are in front of you and behind you. They stay with you, and guard you in accordance with **Allah**'s commands. Thus, **Allah** does not change the condition of any people unless they themselves make the decision to change. If **Allah** wills any hardship for any people, no force can stop it. For they have none beside Him as Lord and Master."*

I think it is safe to say 99% of our earth's population no longer wishes for <u>white authority's</u> 6,000 year old world politics and the New is not yet fully in place. [Hosea 12] *"[1] <u>Ephraim</u> feeds on the wind; he pursues the east wind all day and multiplies <u>lies and violence</u>. He makes a treaty with Assyria and sends olive oil to Egypt. [2] The L<small>ORD</small> has a charge to bring against <u>Judah</u>; he will punish <u>Jacob</u> according to his ways and repay him according to his deeds. [3] In the womb he grasped his brother's heel; as a man he struggled with God. He struggled with the angel and overcame him; he wept and begged for his favor. He found him at Bethel and talked with him there—[5] the L<small>ORD</small> God Almighty, the L<small>ORD</small> is his name! [6] But you must return to your God; maintain love and justice, and wait for your God always. [7] <u>The merchant uses dishonest scales and loves to defraud</u>. [8] Ephraim boasts, "I am very rich; I have become wealthy. With all my wealth they will not find in me any iniquity or sin." [9] "I have been the L<small>ORD</small> your God ever since you came out of Egypt; I will make you live in tents again, as in the days of your appointed festivals. [10] I spoke to* *the prophets, gave them many visions and told parables through them." ¹¹ Is Gilead wicked? Its people are worthless! Do they sacrifice bulls in Gilgal? Their altars will be like piles of stones on a plowed field. ¹² Jacob fled to the country of Aram; Israel served to get a wife, and to pay for her he tended sheep. ¹³ The LORD used a prophet to bring Israel up from Egypt, by a prophet he cared for him. ¹⁴* **But Ephraim has aroused his bitter anger; his Lord will leave on him the guilt of his bloodshed and will repay him for his contempt."**

So as we are Transitioning into The New, billions of people are qualifying for positions awaiting them.

"Big fields are awaiting for the wide Awake man to work out." [33]

Appendix 1

Minister Bey Muhammad

"In the book *Message To The Blackman*, on page 211, under a section entitled "The Persecution of the Righteous," The Most Honorable Elijah Muhammad wrote:

"If Troy X Cade [as he was called before receiving the holy name Abdul Bey Muhammad] is guilty of teaching insurrection against the government, then I am guilty, because I am Troy's teacher. I would rather go to prison in place of Troy if this is the justice for the truth Allah gave me."

"Sentenced to six years in prison in the Louisiana State Penitentiary; isolated from other inmates; forced to sleep on a concrete floor and drink from a commode in his cell; Minister Bey awaited a Louisiana Supreme Court Decision to overturn his conviction.

"Before this decision would take place, however; prison guards, at approximately two o'clock one morning, removed Minister Bey from his cell, shackled him, and turned him over to police and state troopers who drove him to the Louisiana/Mississippi state line.

"Once there, Minister Bey was again brutally beaten within an inch of his life by scores of officers who then attempted to drown him by standing on his body in a swamp until they thought he was dead.
"Only his faith in Allah kept Minister Bey alive, and the fact that he had been a lifeguard, a frogman, and an excellent swimmer with the ability to hold his breath under water.

"After the officers left, Minister Bey crawled out of the swamp onto the highway, where he lay across the pavement, bleeding and severely injured, hoping that someone would stop and help him.

"One of the first Black drivers ever hired to drive for the Greyhound Bus Company was the first to come upon Minister Bey's body on the highway.

"The Driver, along with fellow passengers, helped Minister Bey onto the bus, after which they took him to a medical facility on the Jackson State College (now known as Jackson State University) campus in Mississippi to be treated.

"The Honorable Elijah Muhammad, upon being notified of the incident, sent for Minister Bey to come to his home in Chicago, where, soon after, he stood Minister Bey before the world during the Nation of Islam's Annual Saviour's Day Convention to show what had happened.

"The Honorable Elijah Muhammad then asked Minister Bey to return to prison until the rendering of his Supreme Court Decision, and without hesitation, Minister Bey obeyed. This was to deter any authorities of charging Minister Bey of "escape from prison" in addition to his other convictions which were on appeal.

"Surprisingly, one of the attorneys retained to represent Minister Bey by the Nation of Islam was a member of the Ku Klux Klan; James R. Venable. Mr. Venable wrote a letter to then Attorney General Bobby Kennedy on the Muslims' behalf, and in 1963 at the conclusion of the case, Minister Bey received a favorable ruling from the Louisiana Supreme Court, which overturned his prior convictions.

"Minister Bey is a pioneer in Islam who survived a lynching and beatings born out of religious persecution. We are able to practice Islam freely in the United States today because of Muslims who suffered and persevered; whose steadfast faith in Almighty God Allah, His Messenger and Islam are an example for us to follow for the struggles we face today."[48]

---

[48] www.finalcall.com/artman/publish/National_News_2/article_7342.shtml]

Appendix 2

By elements of where power is held

Aristarchic attributes: Governments with *Aristarchy* attributes are traditionally ruled by the "best" people.

Secret Governments: An interlocking network of official functionaries, spies, mercenaries, ex-generals, profiteers and superpatriots, who, for a variety of motives, operate outside the legitimate institutions of government are traditionally ruled by the "worst" people.

Term	Definition
Aristocracy	Rule by elite citizens; a system of governance in which a person who rules in an aristocracy is an aristocrat. It has come to mean rule by "the aristocracy" who are people of noble birth. An aristocracy is a government by the "best" people. A person who rules in an aristocracy is an aristocrat. Aristocracy is different from nobility, in that nobility means that one bloodline would rule, an aristocracy would mean that a few or many bloodlines would rule, or that rulers be chosen in a different manner.
Geniocracy	Rule by the intelligent; a system of governance where creativity, innovation, intelligence and wisdom are required for those who wish to govern.
Kratocracy	Rule by the strong; a system of governance where those strong enough to seize power through physical force, social maneuvering or political cunning.
Meritocracy	Rule by the meritorious; a system of governance where groups are selected on the basis of people's ability, knowledge in a given area, and contributions to society.

Technocracy	Rule by the educated; a system of governance where people who are skilled or proficient govern in their respective areas of expertise in technology would be in control of all decision making. Doctors, engineers, scientists, professionals and technologists who have knowledge, expertise, or skills, would compose the governing body, instead of politicians, businessmen, and economists.[6] In a technocracy, decision makers would be selected based upon how knowledgeable and skillful they are in their field.

Autocratic attributes

Governments with *Autocratic* attributes are ruled by one person who has all the power over the people in a country. The Roman Republic made *Dictators* to lead during times of war. The Roman dictators (and Greek tyrants) were not always bad. The Roman dictators only held power for a small time. In modern times, an Autocrat's rule is not stopped by any rules of law, constitutions, or other social and political institutions. After World War II, many governments in Latin America, Asia, and Africa were ruled by autocratic governments..

Term	Definition
Authoritarian	Rule by authoritarian governments are characterized by an emphasis on the authority of the state in a republic or union. It is a political system controlled by unelected rulers who usually permit some degree of individual freedom.
Autocracy	Rule by one individual, whose decisions are subject to neither external legal restraints nor regularized mechanisms of popular control (except perhaps for implicit threat). Autocrat needs servants while despot needs slaves.
Despotism	Rule by a single entity with absolute power. That entity may be an individual, as in an autocracy, or it may be a group,[1] as in an oligarchy. The word despotism means to "rule in the fashion of a despot" and does not necessarily require a single, or individual, "despot". Despot needs slaves while Autocrat needs servants.
Dictatorship	Rule by an individual who has full power over the country. The term may refer to a system where the dictator came to power, and holds it, purely by force; but it also includes systems where the

dictator first came to power legitimately but then was able to amend the constitution so as to, in effect, gather all power for themselves. In a military dictatorship, the army is in control. Usually, there is little or no attention to public opinion or individual rights. See also Autocracy and Stratocracy.

Fascism	Rule by leader base only. Focuses heavily on patriotism and national identity. The leader(s) has the power to make things illegal that do not relate to nationalism, or increase belief in national pride. They believe their nation is based on commitment to an organic national community where its citizens are united together as one people through a national identity. It exalts nation and race above the individual and stands for severe economic and social regimentation, and forcible suppression of opposition.
Totalitarian	Rule by a totalitarian government that regulates nearly every aspect of public and private life.

Democratic attributes

Governments with *Democratic* attributes are most common in the Western world and in some countries of the east. In democracies, all of the people in a country can vote during elections for representatives or political parties that they prefer. The people in democracies can elect representatives who will sit on legislatures such as the Parliament or Congress. Political parties are organizations of people with similar ideas about how a country or region should be governed. Different political parties have different ideas about how the government should handle different problems. Democracy is the government of the people, by the people, for the people.

Term	Definition
Democracy	Rule by a government chosen by election where most of the populace are enfranchised. The key distinction between a democracy and other forms of constitutional government is usually taken to be that the right to vote is not limited by a person's wealth or race (the main qualification for enfranchisement is usually having reached a certain age). A Democratic government is, therefore, one supported (at least at the time of the election) by a majority of the populace (provided the election was held fairly). A "majority" may be

defined in different ways. There are many "power-sharing" (usually in countries where people mainly identify themselves by race or religion) or "electoral-college" or "constituency" systems where the government is not chosen by a simple one-vote-per-person headcount.

<u>Direct democracy</u>	Government in which the people represent themselves and vote directly for new laws and public policy
<u>Representative democracy</u>	Also known as a republic, wherein the people or citizens of a country elect representatives to create and implement public policy in place of active participation by the people.
<u>Social democracy</u>	Social democracy rejects the "either/or" polarization interpretation of capitalism versus socialism. It claims that fostering a progressive evolution of capitalism will gradually result in the evolution of capitalist economy into socialist economy. Social democracy argues that all citizens should be legally entitled to certain social rights. These are made up of universal access to public services such as: education, health care, workers' compensation, and other services including child care and care for the elderly. Social democracy is connected with the trade union labour movement and supports collective bargaining rights for workers. Contemporary social democracy advocates freedom from discrimination based on differences of: ability/disability, age, ethnicity, gender, language, race, religion, sexual orientation, and social class.

Monarchic attributes

Governments with *Monarchic* attributes are ruled by a king or a queen who inherits their position from their family, which is often called the "royal family." There are at two opposing types of monarchies: absolute monarchies and constitutional monarchies. In an absolute monarchy, the ruler has no limits on their wishes or powers. In a constitutional monarchy a ruler's powers are limited by a document called a constitution. The constitution was put in place to put a check to these powers

Term	Definition

Term	Definition
Absolute monarchy	Rule by a government in which a monarch exercises ultimate governing authority as head of state and head of government.
Constitutional monarchy	Rule by a government that has a monarch, but one whose powers are limited by law or by a formal constitution, such as that in the United Kingdom.
Elective monarchy	Rule by a government that has an elected monarch, in contrast to a *hereditary monarchy* in which the office is automatically passed down as a family inheritance. The manner of election, the nature of candidate qualifications, and the electors vary from case to case.
Emirate	Similar to a monarchy or sultanate, but a government in which the supreme power is in the hands of an emir (the ruler of a Muslim state); the emir may be an absolute overlord or a sovereign with constitutionally limited authority.[1]
Monarchy	Rule by an individual who has inherited the role and expects to bequeath it to their heir.

Oligarchic attributes

Governments with *Oligarchic* attributes are ruled by a small group of powerful and/or influential people. These people may spread power equally or not equally. An oligarchy is different from a true democracy because very few people are given the chance to change things. An oligarchy does not have to be hereditary or monarchic. An oligarchy does not have one clear ruler, but several powerful people. Some historical examples of oligarchy are the former Union of Soviet Socialist Republics and Apartheid in South Africa. Some critics of representative democracy think of the United States as an oligarchy. This view is shared by anarchists.

Term	Definition
Bureaucracy	Rule by a system of governance with many bureaus, administrators, and petty officials
Ergatocracy	Rule by a system of governance ruled by proletariats, the workers, or the working class. Examples of ergatocracy include communist revolutionaries & rebels which control almost society and create

	alternative economy for people's and workers. See <u>Dictatorship of the proletariat</u>.
<u>Kritarchy</u>	Rule by judges; a system of governance composed of law enforcement institutions in which the state and the <u>legal systems</u> are traditionally the same thing.
<u>Netocracy</u>	Rule by social connections; a term invented by the editorial board of the American technology magazine Wired in the early 1990s. A portmanteau of Internet and aristocracy, netocracy refers to a perceived global upper-class that bases its power on a technological advantage and networking skills, in comparison to what is portrayed as a bourgeoisie of a gradually diminishing importance. The netocracy concept has been compared with <u>Richard Florida</u>'s concept of the <u>creative class</u>. Bard and Söderqvist have also defined an under-class in opposition to the <u>netocracy</u>, which they refer to as the <u>consumtariat</u>.
<u>Oligarchy</u>	Rule by a system of governance with small group of people who share similar interests or family relations.
<u>Plutocracy</u>	Rule by the rich; a system of governance composed of the wealthy class. Any of the forms of government listed here can be plutocracy. For instance, if all of the voted representatives in a republic are wealthy, then it is a republic and a plutocracy.
<u>Stratocracy</u>	Rule by military service; a system of governance composed of military government in which the state and the military are traditionally the same thing. Citizens with military service have the right to govern. (Not to be confused with "<u>military junta</u>" or "<u>military dictatorship</u>".)
<u>Timocracy</u>	Rule by honor; a system of governance ruled by honorable citizens and property owners. European-feudalism and post-Revolutionary America are historical examples of this type.
<u>Theocracy</u>	Rule by a religious elite; a system of governance composed of religious institutions in which the state and the church are traditionally the same thing. Citizens who are clergy have the right

to govern. The Vatican's (see Pope)

Pejorative attributes

Regardless of whichever forms of government a nation, and its people, may choose for themselves; all must be safeguarded against passion and corruption. A democracy spoiled by demagoguery can become a *Mobocracy*. An aristocracy spoiled by corruption can become an "Oligarchy. *A monarchy spoiled by lack of virtue can become tyrannical.*

Term	Definition
Bankocracy	Rule by banks; a system of governance where the excessive power or influence of banks on public policy-making. It can also refer to a form of government where financial institutions rule society. See Trapezocracy.
Corporatocracy	Rule by corporations; a system of governance where an economic and political system is controlled by corporations or corporate interests. Its use is generally pejorative. Fictional examples include *OCP* in Robocop
Nepotocracy	Rule by nephews; favoritism granted to relatives regardless of merit; a system of governance in which importance is given to the relatives of those already in power, like a *nephew* (where the word comes from). In such governments even if the relatives aren't qualified they are given positions of authority just because they know someone who already has authority. Pope Alexander VI (Borgia) was accused of this.
Kakistocracy	Rule by the stupid; a system of governance where the worst or least-qualified citizens govern or dictate policies. See Idiocracy.
Kleptocracy (Mafia state)	Rule by thieves; a system of governance where its officials and the ruling class in general pursue personal wealth and political power at the expense of the wider population. In strict terms kleptocracy is not a form of government but a *characteristic* of a government engaged in such behavior. Examples include Mexico as being considered a *Narcokleptocracy*, since its democratic government is perceived to be corrupted by those

	who profit from trade in illegal drugs smuggled into the United States.
Ochlocracy	Rule by the general populace; a system of governance where mob rule is government by mob or a mass of people, or the intimidation of legitimate authorities. As a pejorative for majoritarianism, it is akin to the Latin phrase *mobile vulgus* meaning "the fickle crowd", from which the English term "mob" was originally derived in the 1680s. Ochlocratic goverments are often a democracy spoiled by demagoguery, "tyranny of the majority" and the rule of passion over reason; such governments can be *more oppressive* then autocratic-Tyrants. Ochlocracy is synonymous in meaning and usage to the modern, informal term "Mobocracy," which emerged from a much more recent colloquial etymology.

Other characteristic attributes

Term	Definition
Adhocracy	Rule by a government based on type of organization that operates in opposite fashion to a bureaucracy.
Anarchism	Sometimes said to be non-governance; it is a structure which strives for non-hierarchical voluntary associations among agents.
Band Society	Rule by a government based on small (usually family) unit with a semi-informal hierarchy, with strongest (either physical strength or strength of character) as leader. Very much like a pack seen in other animals, such as wolves.
Chiefdom (Tribal)	Rule by a government based on small complex society of varying degrees of centralization that is led by an individual known as a chief.
Constitutional republic	Rule by a government whose powers are limited by law or a formal constitution, and chosen by a vote amongst at least some sections of the populace (Ancient Sparta was in its own terms a republic, though most inhabitants were disenfranchised. The

United States is a federal republic). Republics that exclude sections of the populace from participation will typically claim to represent all citizens (by defining people without the vote as "non-citizens").

Cybersynacy — Ruled by a data fed group of secluded individuals that regulates aspects of public and private life using data feeds and technology having no interactivity with the citizens but using "facts only" to decide direction.

Nomocracy — Rule by a government under the sovereignty of rational laws and civic right as opposed to one under theocratic systems of government. In a nomocracy, ultimate and final authority (sovereignty) exists in the law.

Republic — Rule by a form of government in which the people, or some significant portion of them, have supreme control over the government and where offices of state are elected or chosen by elected people. In modern times, a common simplified definition of a republic is a government where the head of state is not a monarch. Montesquieu included both democracies, where all the people have a share in rule, and aristocracies or oligarchies, where only some of the people rule, as republican forms of government.

Term	Definition

Magocracy — Rule by a government ruled by the highest and main authority being either a magician, sage, sorcerer, wizard or witch. This is often similar to a theocratic structured regime and is largely portrayed in fiction and fantasy genre categories.

Uniocracy — Ruled by a singularity of all human minds connected via some form of technical or non technical telepathy acting as a form of super computer to make decisions based on shared patterned experiences to deliver fair and accurate decisions to problems as they arrive. Also known as the hive mind principle, differs from voting in that each person would make a decision while in the "hive" the synapses of all minds work together following a longer path of memories to make "one" decision.

By socio-economic attributes

Historically, most political systems originated as socio-economic movements; experience with those movements in power, and the strong ties they may have to particular forms of government, can cause them to be considered as forms of government in themselves.

Term	Definition
Capitalism	In a capitalist or free-market economy, people own their own businesses and property and must buy services for private use, such as healthcare.
Communism	In a communist country, the government owns all businesses and farms and provides its people's healthcare, education and welfare.
Feudalism	A system of land ownership and duties. Under feudalism, all the land in a kingdom was the king's. However, the king would give some of the land to the lords or nobles who fought for him. These presents of land were called manors. Then the nobles gave some of their land to vassals. The vassals then had to do duties for the nobles. The lands of vassals were called fiefs.
Socialism	Socialist government's own many of the larger industries and provide education, health and welfare services while allowing citizens some economic choices
Welfare state	**Concept of government in which the state plays a key role in the protection and promotion of the economic and social well-being of its citizens. It is based on the principles of equality of opportunity, equitable distribution of wealth, and public responsibility for those unable to avail themselves of the minimal provisions for a good life.**

Appendix 3

Six Thousand Year Transition of Nations

The biblical story about how the original nation of peace and righteousness was overthrown in the Holy City Mecca, Arabia over 6,000 years ago is cryptically found in the Bible book of Genesis. However, by the time we get to the last book of the Bible—Revelations 21-22, another new world of peace and righteousness begins to transition back to its original status to endure without end. It is known as the Kingdom of God, New Jerusalem, and Heaven on Earth or Universal Government of Peace. The new begins in the West. Many symbolic biblical passages have been used to represent the nature of a New Government that is going to be ruled by God's new chosen people. [Jeremiah 3:15-18]

Just as the old world of Satan has been ruled and dominated by men and women with government and financial knowledge, the New Government of God is also ruled by human beings—men and women. The question is: will the NEW be ruled by the Black man and women of America as taught by Honorable Elijah Muhammad? THAT IS THE 64 MILLION DOLLAR QUESTION! Who will be at its SEAT[S] OF AUTHORITY!

Over the past 6,600 years, our ancient Black and Red civilizations have undergone a process or a period changing from one state or condition to another. That is, the governments of the original people once lived in peace before devolving from peace into war, lies and deceit. The Christian Bible describes this transitional period as the

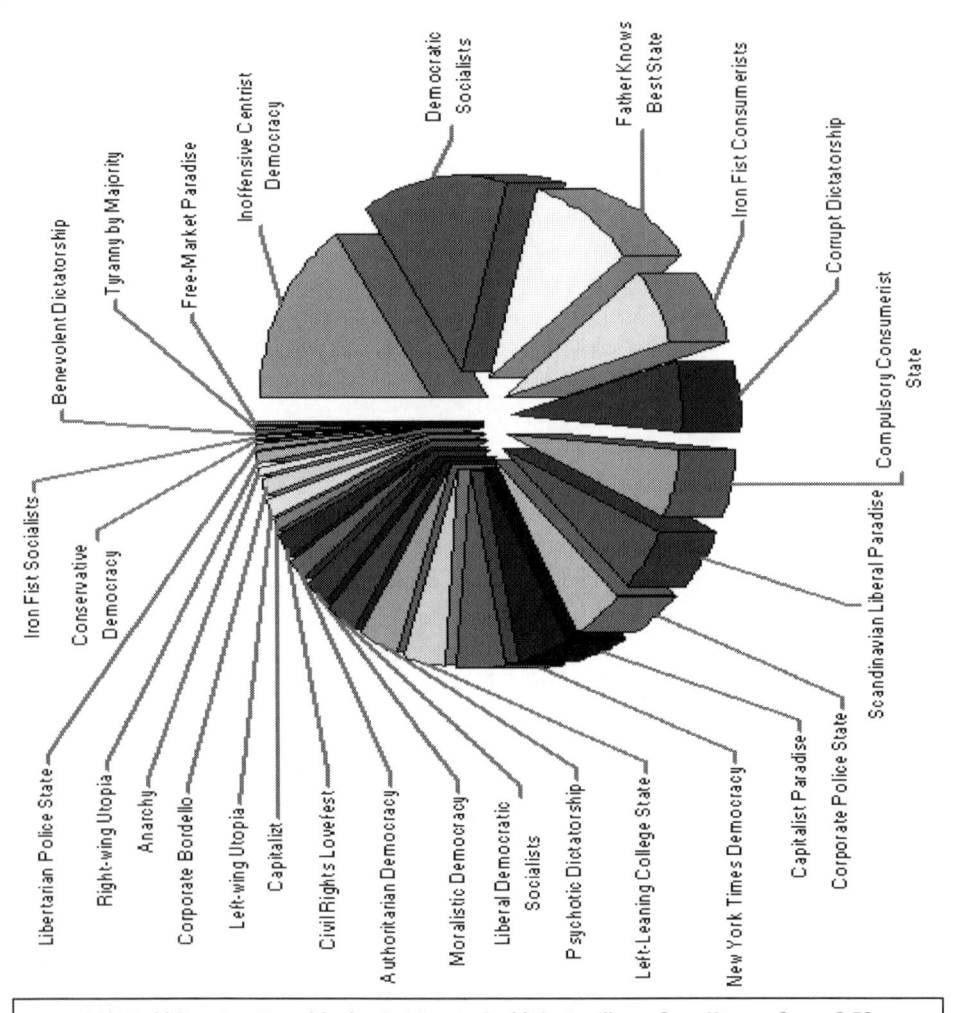

Old World Structure Transitioning Out Due to Covid19—Pestilence from Heaven Quran 2:59

Inoffensive Centrist Democracy is the most popular nation type, comprising just over 15% of all nations. It's closely followed by *Democratic Socialists*, with about 14%.

Interestingly, you have to get down to #6 on the list, *Compulsory Consumerist State*, before you find a nation type with more freedom on any scale than the middle-of-the-road *Inoffensive Centrist Democracy* -- and even then it's economic freedom at the expense of personal freedom. The first nation type to be clearly more liberty-loving than the default is *Capitalist Paradise* (#9). [Source: **NationStates | Analysis of Nations by UN Classification** fall of man. This fall began in the east or biblical "Garden of Eden" where the original civilization once upheld righteousness as the rule of law.

Murder, lies and deceit became the order of the day over 6,000 years ago introduced by a new race of people. The name of God, the Bible does not give us before the fall of the original nation in EDEN that ruled before the so-white race or new race. Moreover, the form of government set in place before their rule, the Bible does not define except the say *Garden of Eden* i.e. heaven on earth.[50]

Whereas the center of authority for spiritual and technical guidance once permeated from many ancient governments of the east from Mecca to Egypt to Sumer and Elam, down the wheel of time, these centers of power governments of the east and Asia Minor eventually were overcome by western Caucasians—whom where biblically hidden under the name Satan. [Revelation 13:2]

For example: they set up in ancient Rome, then into England and finally into North America. This transition of authority mainly began around 300 AD and finally settled under white authority in 1776, July 4th. As you can see, in between these transitions from one government and its citizens to next, centuries of time passed, millions of lives were lost and wars prosecuted to bring about white authority.

The Honorable Elijah Muḥammad taught:

The Black Man[s] Gods, according to the history He taught me, have All been the Wisest. They made the white man after their order in wisdom except the knowledge of how to bring into reality and perfection their vision and idea of what they want to perceive equal to the Black Mans Wisdom. This was kept back. They are forced to build their world on

---

[50] Land area of ancient Arabia, Egypt and Mesopotamia.

the basis of what they found in the Wisdom of Black Man. The white man only made, formed, and put into service those things that met with the cravings and necessities of his people. The white man was given the power of vision and different ways of life to enable him to build an unalike world from what we have had throughout the millions, billions, and trillions of years. No God Who is going to rule the people of earth universally, as the white man has ruled for the past six thousand years, was to be given a history or knowledge of the God Who ruled the people before Him. This is in order to keep the Present God from patterning after the Former God and to force Him to use His Own Wisdom in making a world and not a world patterning after previous Wisdom of the Gods Before Him. The white race did not get a chance to rule solely according to their wisdom because we were present and they patterned much of their world after what they saw of the Gods of the Black Man. This was due to the fact that the white race was made an enemy to the Black Man; therefore their time to deceive the Black Man was limited to a short span of six thousand years that are used by the Black Gods to rule.[51]

Civilizations and governments have advanced from horse and chariot, to automobiles and planes, from gold and coin currency to paper money and electronic currency. But, nothing has been new under the sun, over the past 6,000 years, except a fully fledged establishment and commercialization of depravity under what the righteous identified as Satanic rules of law.

Again, according to the teachings of the Honorable Elijah Muhammad, a new world of deceit came into existence 6,000 years ago. This new world was fully manifested through the making of the white race by their father Yakub [Genesis 1:26; Holy Quran 2:30-32].

Western civilization—America and Europe—and their entire agent states are the result of what Yakub's made race

---

[51] http://muhammadspeaks.com/home/?page_id=862

envisioned from one era to the next by using war and bloodshed under the tutelage of the Talmud[52]—some of the forgotten Tricknology of Yakub. One might say Yakub was their first sage.

Therefore, in a step by step transitional process, the white race tricked and battered the original righteous nations of the earth into submission under the barrel of a gun, a bomb or a financial debt instrument. However, such world is ending, now we crave the NEW. This is the time, so what must be done?

---

[52] ...the word "talmud"—generally in the phrase "talmud lomar"—is frequently used in tannaitic terminology in order to denote instruction by means of the text of the Bible and of the exegetic deductions therefrom. ... the noun "talmud" has the meaning which alone can be genetically connected with the name "Talmud"; in tannaitic phraseology the verb "limmed" denotes the exegetic deduction of a halakic principle from the Biblical text ...into which the study of the traditional exegesis of the Bible was from earliest times of the sages....[of the Caucasian Jews.]

Appendix 4

U.S. Debt Clock August 14, 2021 12:07 PM

	Debt or Savings	*In the last* 89 secs.
Borrowed by the General Fund	− $ 28,640,067,900,382*	$ 3,234,048
Debt Per Citizen		+ $ 85,870
US Total Debt		+ $ 85,619,841,899,999

*Gross National Debt ♦ †Debt Held by the Public ♦ Debt Clock
Source Data August, 2021 12:07 pm

End Notes

1. http://en.wikipedia.org/wiki/Civic_duties] pg. 24
2. See Appendix 1: Elements of where power is Held pg. 25
3. http://en.wikipedia.org/wiki/Corporatocracy pg. 27
4. http://www.noi.org/about.shtml pg. 34
5. http://www.thenationofislam.org/supremewisdom.html pg. 44
6. http://en.wikipedia.org/wiki/Vatican_City pg. 46
7. http://www.thenationofislam.org/supremewisdom.html pg. 48
8. http://en.wikipedia.org/wiki/Consent_of_the_governed Pg. 54
9. http://www.constitutionofmadina.com/ pg. 65
10. http://en.wikipedia.org/wiki/Minister_(government)#Etymology pg. 79
11. [source: http://www.thenationofislam.org/supremewisdom.html] pg. 80
12. http://www.thenationofislam.org/supremewisdom.html pg. 82
13. http://www.thenationofislam.org/supremewisdom.html pg. 83
14. http://www.thenationofislam.org/supremewisdom.html pg. 84
15. http://www.thenationofislam.org/supremewisdom.html pg. 84
16. http://www.thenationofislam.org/supremewisdom.html pg. 84
17. http://www.thenationofislam.org/supremewisdom.html pg. 87
18. http://www.thenationofislam.org/supremewisdom.html pg. 93
19. http://www.thenationofislam.org/supremewisdom.html pg. 94
20. http://www.thenationofislam.org/supremewisdom.html pg. 94
21. http://en.wikipedia.org/wiki/Dialect pg. 95
22. http://www.thenationofislam.org/supremewisdom.html pg. 96
23. http://www.thenationofislam.org/supremewisdom.html] pg. 97
24. http://www.thenationofislam.org/supremewisdom.html pg. 100
25. http://www.thenationofislam.org/supremewisdom.html pg. 111
26. http://www.thenationofislam.org/supremewisdom.html pg. 112
27. http://www.thenationofislam.org/supremewisdom.html pg. 112
28. http://www.finalcall.com/national/savioursday2k/hem_nation.htm pg. 118
29. http://www.finalcall.com/artman/publish/World_News_3/article_8790.shtml pg. 130
30. http://www.noiwc.org/nationofislamcaribbean.html pg. 135
31. http://www.thenationofislam.org/supremewisdom.html pg. 136
32. The Federation of the West Indies (1958-1962) pg.147
33. http://www.thenationofislam.org/supremewisdom.html pg. 112

Recommended Reading

Brief Biography Rasheed L. Muhammad

At the age 10, during the 1970's Brother Rasheed (AKA Anthony X Perry) and his siblings attended Muhammad University of Islam #8, San Diego, California under Brother minister Amos. My mother, Sister Doris X was a Lieutenant over the MGT & GCC and had the privileged to spend seven day's at the Palace of the Nation of Islam to meet with the Honorable Elijah Muhammad regarding certain business matters vis-à-vis MGT garment production.

After the fall of the Nation of Islam in 1975, his father settled on choosing the last name Rasheed. From 1975 to 1981, Rasheed attended public schools and completed one year of college before being expelled from grade-13 for being too militant and un-coachable. Upon his return to San Diego, California he was blessed to attend a meeting convened by brother Akbar Muhammad (formerly known as Larry X) and the late Dr. Khaild Muhammad (former known as Harold X) to establish a study group at the home of Sister Irene X and brother James E. X Robinson. In 1981, he also had the honor to sit face to face with Minister Farrakhan downtown San Diego, at Jack-n-the Box. Rasheed recalls looking at the Minister saying, "teach me all about Egypt"...after staring back for a moment, the Minister replied, "read all the books of the Honorable Elijah Muhammad first, and then I will teach you."

After helping to establish San Diego's first study group, at the age of 19, brother Rasheed moved into the FOI house and assisted then minister Harvey X Robinson to "push Muhammad's Program" under the leadership of the Honorable Minister Louis Farrakhan. At that time all study guides were provided by Minister Jabril Muhammad of Mosque #32.

In 1982, he decided to relocate to Los Angeles, California after attending several FOI classes under the Captainship of Abdul Malik Muhammad and the ministry of the late Dr. Khalid Muhammad (RIP).

He eventually moved into the basement of the Muhammad Mosque #27, along with numerous other FOI, and became a part of an around the clock team of soldiers by day, worked at night and maintained various Mosque security details seven days per week. Over the years, he served as Final Call Paper captain, studied in Jabril Muhammad's ministry class, and taught Islam on several Wednesday nights for student ministers in training during the year 1984.

In 1985, he met the acquaintance of Rasul Hakim Muhammad (son of the Honorable Elijah Muhammad), who lived with him on and off for two years, at his apartment which served as a FOI living location. Through this relationship, he was introduced to Mr. Jim Brown by Rasul who suggested to brother Rasheed, "stick" with Jim Brown". In 1986, he also had the privilege to chauffer Mother Tynetta Muhammad to a variety of events throughout Los Angeles during the year 1986-87 cultivating much wisdom she divulged and read books she recommended.

In 1988, while at Mosque 27, not only did Rasheed rank third in raising funds behind Sultan Muhammad (former known as Gregory X) to help recoup Muhammad Mosque #2, he also laid to grass around Mosque Maryam in 1989.

Around 1990, Rasheed began working with Jim Browns Street Organization Intervention Program thanks to Tarik Ross (a nephew of Minster Louis Farrakhan).

In 1992, Rasheed was asked by several Street Organization leaders to prepare a peace treaty for the so-called gangs of Watts, California. On June 17, 1992 the truce document and what the Watts Street Organizations were trying to achieve made Los Angeles Time Headline news.

"Ex-Gang Members Look to Mideast for a Peace Plan : Truce: Group uses 1949 cease-fire agreement between Egypt and Israel as the basis for an agreement among L.A.'s Bloods and Crips." **June 17, 1992**/*JESSE KATZ and ANDREA FORD | TIMES STAFF WRITERS*

From 1991 to 2001, Rasheed traveled to nineteen states and numerous cities teaching and training Life Skills Education for Jim Browns **I-Can Program** in schools, juvenile detention centers and prisons from Harlem to Brooklyn New York to Northeast Portland to Miami, Florida from Canton, Ohio to Texas.

In 2006 he implemented a nationhood educational curriculum for Muhammad University of Islam Mosque #54 under former University Director, Brandon Muhammad.

In 2007, he acquired a California Real Estate License, 2012 received his Mortgage Math and Underwriter Certificate.

Lastly, since 1995 Rasheed L Muhammad has published 37 books (24 written after 2008).

Books by Rasheed L. Muhammad

1) Minister Farrakhan Revealed In Black and White
2) The Real Niggers: Oops Did I Say Niggards **(Removed by Amazon)**
3) The Mathematical Parable of 19: Allah (God's) Holy Number
4) Farrakhan The Jesus Factor: Vol. 1, 13 Chapter Curriculum
5) FARRAKHAN The Jesus FACTOR Vol. 2 Book Version
6) Islamic Studies To Black Women and the 7 Churches
7) The Classical Gold Standard: Fall of Caucasian Civilization
8) Nation Of Islam Decoded: Sciences of Mankind
9) The Pork Report Cat, Rat and Dog **(Removed by Amazon)**
10) The Original Gang Truce Of 1992
11) Black Nation Mother and Father of Civilization
12) Supreme Wisdom for Developing Nations and Black America
13) Quran Verse: Out with the Old in with the New 1975–2012—2015
14) Secrets Of The Holy City Mecca, Arabia Vol. 1
15) Secrets Of The Holy City Mecca, Arabia Vol. 2
16) The Truth
17) The Federal Reserve System: In God We Trust
18) Black people White people: Who is the Devil
19) Power of Zionism: A 6,000 Year Journey To White Control
20) Jesus is a Black Man
21) Ancient Wisdom of the Nation of Islam
22) The Black Women: Her Divine Nature Vol.1
23) The Black Women: Her Divine Nature Vol. 2
24) Message To Hip Hop: Get Your Conscious Back
25) Allah is a God: Alllaah Is The Supreme Being Vol. 1
26) Our Brain and 9 Systems Equal Physio Economics of God: The Divine Knowledge of God-Self
27) Book Of Yakub: Father Of The White Race
28. Who Is The Honorable Minister Louis Farrakhan
29. My Testamony To Minister Farrakhan: Highlights of Muhammad's Temple #27
30. Black Muslim Wife and Husband
31. What He Revealed: Title and Deeds of the Universe Vol. 1
32. Introduction To A Study of Government: Civic Engagement & 10 Community Ministries.
33. Separation: Benefits of Building Our Community
34. Movie Script---Mr. Yakub
35. Movie Script---True History of Jesus 2000 Years Ago

Made in the USA
Columbia, SC
13 October 2021